LOST RAILWAYS
OF SOUTH & WEST
YORKSHIRE

Gordon Suggitt

COUNTRYSIDE BOOKS
NEWBURY, BERKSHIRE

First published 2007
© Gordon Suggitt 2007

All rights reserved. No reproduction
permitted without the prior permission
of the publisher:

COUNTRYSIDE BOOKS
3 Catherine Road
Newbury, Berkshire

To view our complete range of books,
please visit us at
www.countrysidebooks.co.uk

ISBN 978 1 84674 043 5

Designed by Graham Whiteman
Maps and photographs by the author

The cover picture shows ex-LNER class B16 4-6-0 No 61429
at Collingham Bridge station with a Wetherby–Leeds
passenger train in 1961.
(From an original painting by Colin Doggett)

Produced through MRM Associates Ltd., Reading
Typeset by Mac Style, Nafferton, East Yorkshire
Printed by Information Press, Oxford

*All material for the manufacture of this book was
sourced from sustainable forests.*

CONTENTS

ACKNOWLEDGEMENTS

I would like to acknowledge the help and resources provided by
the libraries in South and West Yorkshire. I would also like to
thank individually Allan Wood, David Chatfield, Nick Metcalfe
and M.A. King for the use of their photo collections, Mick
Coulson and Frank Jolliffe for the use of their reminiscences and
Mike Clark for his help with loco identification. Lastly I am yet
again especially grateful to my wife Jen for her encouragement
and help, and particularly for her meticulous checking of the
text.

ABBREVIATIONS

The following abbreviations are used in this book:

BR	British Railways (known as British Rail from late 1960s onwards)
BW&LR	Bradford, Wakefield & Leeds Railway
DMU	Diesel multiple unit
DVR	Dearne Valley Railway
E&WYUR	East & West Yorkshire Union Railway
GCR	Great Central Railway
GER	Great Eastern Railway
GNR	Great Northern Railway
H&B	Hull & Barnsley Railway
H&SJR	Huddersfield & Sheffield Junction Railway
K&WVR	Keighley & Worth Valley Railway
LB&HJR	Leeds, Bradford & Halifax Junction Railway
LD&ECR	Lancashire, Derbyshire & East Coast Railway
LMS	London, Midland & Scottish Railway
LNER	London & North Eastern Railway
LNWR	London & North Western Railway
LYR	Lancashire & Yorkshire Railway
MS&LR	Manchester, Sheffield & Lincolnshire Railway
NER	North Eastern Railway
NMR	North Midland Railway
SA&MR	Sheffield, Ashton-under-Lyne & Manchester Railway
SLJR	South Leeds Junction Railway
SRBWH&GR	Sheffield, Rotherham, Barnsley, Wakefield, Huddersfield & Goole Railway
SYR	South Yorkshire Railway
WRUR	West Riding Union Railway

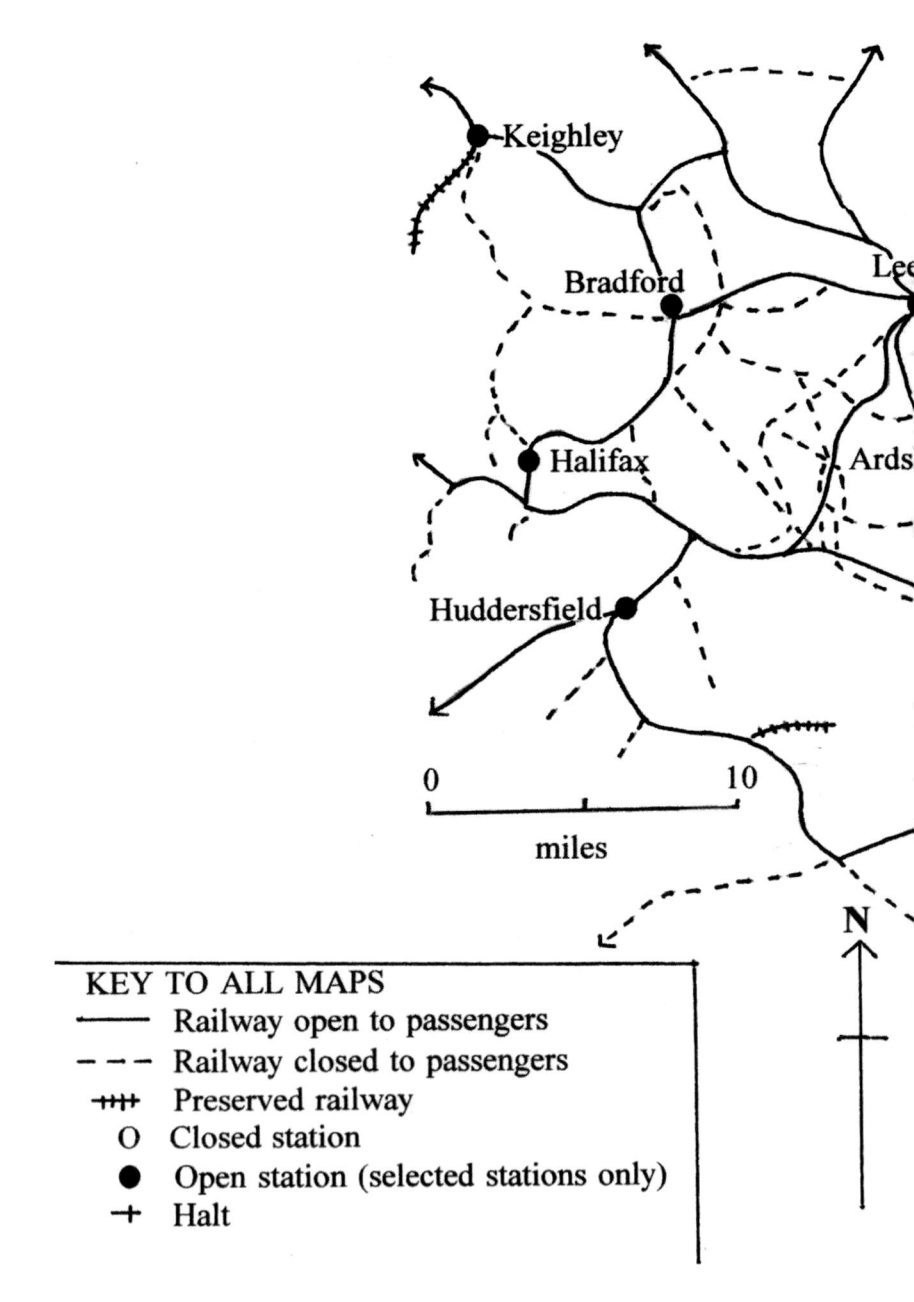

Keighley

Bradford

Le⟨

Halifax

Ards

Huddersfield

0   10

miles

N

KEY TO ALL MAPS
—— Railway open to passengers
- - - Railway closed to passengers
+++ Preserved railway
  O Closed station
  ● Open station (selected stations only)
  + Halt

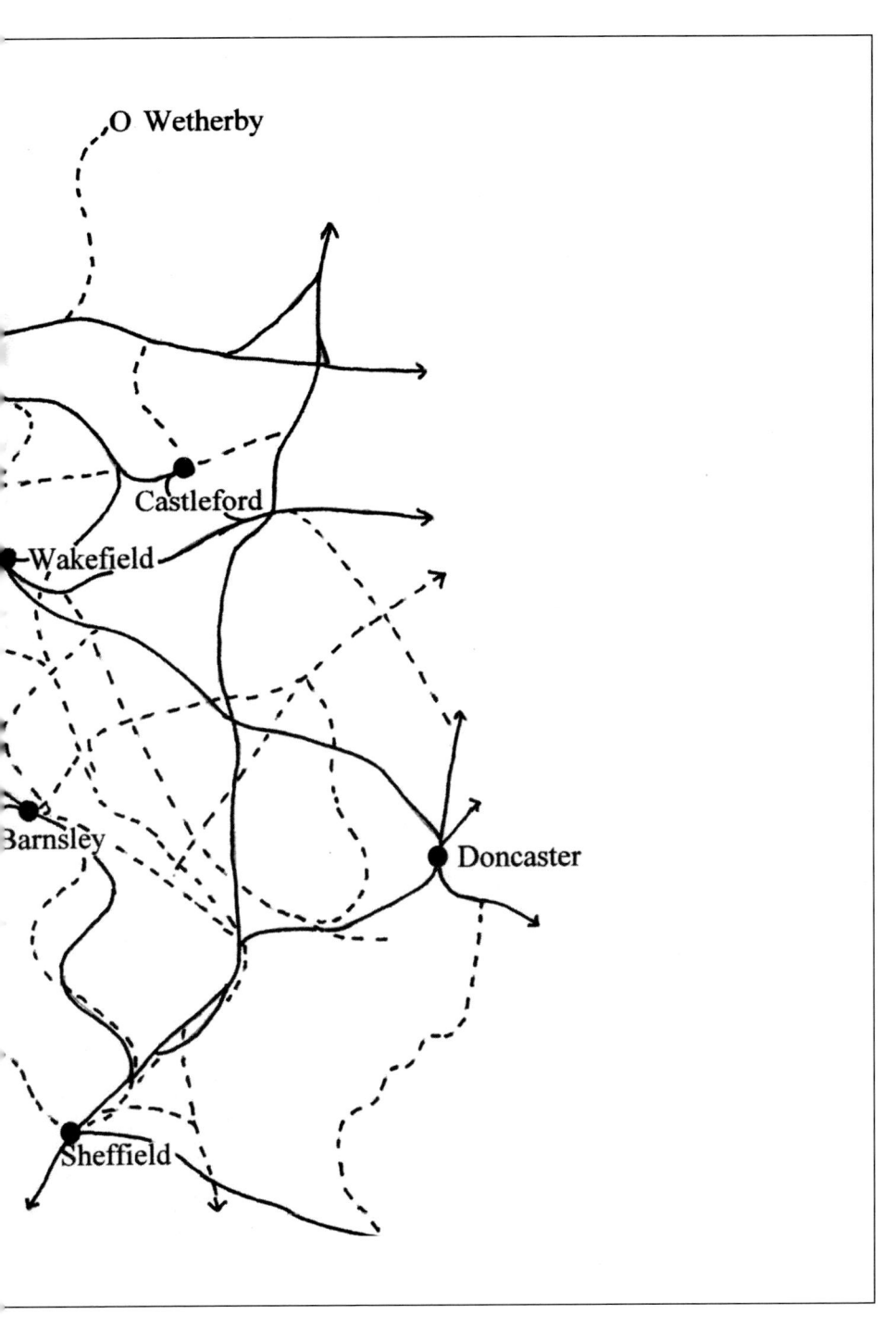
O Wetherby

Castleford

Wakefield

Barnsley

Doncaster

Sheffield

Introduction

Industry! This was the one-word label provided for the then West Riding on Estra Clark's famous map of Yorkshire produced for British Railways in 1949. The caption was accompanied by representations of a miner, a factory worker and a mill hand, together with a steam-hauled passenger train, perhaps suggesting rail services connecting the locations of these industries. Truly rural branches were a rarity, especially in the metropolitan counties of South and West Yorkshire that replaced the West Riding in 1974, as large areas of the Yorkshire Dales formerly in the latter went to North Yorkshire instead. Even the branches away from the main towns and cities were usually built to reach mills, mines and quarries, with only the quite remote branch to Wetherby more akin to those in neighbouring North and East Yorkshire.

It is perhaps the density of the rail network built to cater for the area's industry that has deterred much coverage of its railways as a whole. The introductory map shows particularly dense concentrations of disused lines in the areas east of Barnsley and south-west of Leeds, produced by the efforts of five major pre-Grouping companies (and some independent ones) to capture the trade in wool, coal and steel. Not since David Joy's volume in the *Regional History of the Railways of Great Britain* series first appeared in 1975 has an overall coverage been attempted in books other than collections of photographs. This contrasts with the generous provision of books on individual lines with scarcely a branch not covered, and several such as the Holmfirth branch and the South Yorkshire Joint Railway with at least two titles. This wealth of information at a local level, along with the complexity of the network, has meant that tight guidelines have had to be followed to allow the area's lost railways to be covered in the format of this series.

First, the area of the two former metropolitan counties has been strictly adhered to, with lines heading south from Sheffield and Rotherham left to a coverage of Derbyshire. All freight-only lines have been left out, although those lines built for freight that did manage a passenger service, however short-lived, are included. Only lines with passenger operations after 1900 have been considered, while most spurs and short links have been omitted. More crucially perhaps, most closed terminal stations in the cities have not been included, as they were generally replaced by new stations on or near their sites, and with one exception (Sheffield Victoria) did not form part of a separate line.

Even within these limits there are still 44 or so closed lines to be covered. Consideration was given to a strictly geographical format, as in David Joy's book, but a compromise has been used instead. This gives each pre-Grouping company one or more chapters, while still following a loosely geographical approach. With a few exceptions identified in the text and maps, dealing with the area company by company allows a progression from the north-east corner anti-clockwise round eventually to the east of the region. However, most attention is still given to the individual lines and the passenger services that used them.

So what does this industry-dominated area have to offer in terms of closed passenger lines? The answer is a surprising amount of variety. These lines had passenger services ranging from nine months on a colliery branch at Rothwell to almost 140 years of expresses on the former Midland main line. Sometimes contrasts were dramatically close, for example at Ardsley around 1950, where a portion of the 'West Riding' express from Bradford would pass push-pull services for Castleford – both travelling over lines now gone. All these were well in the future at the start of the historic Middleton Railway, which, although a present-day preserved line, begins this coverage of the area's lost railways.

Gordon Suggitt

1
In the Beginning

The Middleton Railway

Before preservation – colliery loco Blenkinsop, *an 0–6–0 Hudswell Clarke tank built as late as 1954, at work on the Middleton Railway. (P. Wilson)*

Much is made of the parts played in railway history by the Stockton & Darlington and Liverpool & Manchester Railways. Often overlooked are the claims to fame of a small preserved railway in South Leeds. The Middleton Railway can claim to be the world's oldest working railway, and also the subject of the first British Railway Act of Parliament, the home of the world's first commercially successful steam locomotives and Britain's first volunteer-run standard gauge preserved railway.

As early as 1755 a Leeds estate owner, Charles Brandling, obtained leave to build a wooden wagon-way from his coal mines at Middleton to staithes on the River Aire. Three years later he brought a Private Bill before Parliament for a similar wagon-way, this time to the town of Leeds, and it is this second route that is the start of the present-day railway. By 1808 there were 4¼ miles of the Middleton wagon-way system, all horse-drawn, from mines to the staithes at the river and serving Leeds. In that year, John Blenkinsop became Brandling's agent at Middleton, and three years later took out patents for a rack rail system of traction and steam locomotives to use it.

The design of the engine was entrusted to Matthew Murray, a partner in a nearby engineering firm. By 1812 his first locomotives, *Prince Regent* and *Salamanca*, had been tested and were in service on the Middleton system, now reconstructed for the rack rail system. Two years later the Middleton collieries for

Among the early preserved locos was this ex-LNER class Y1 Sentinel shunter, seen in 1973. (Author's collection)

11

the first time had an annual production exceeding 100,000 tons. But by 1835 this was down by 25% and steam traction was abandoned on the Middleton system, which reverted to horse-power. In 1862 it was sold to what became the Middleton Estate and Colliery Company, which reintroduced steam traction, using conventional rails and locos, though on a 4 ft 1 in gauge until 1881. In 1875 the system's main line had been realigned roughly north–south to give the route used by today's trains. This replaced the Belle Isle incline of 1758, worked by a self-acting system with a brake drum.

The main part of the system of 1875 continued in commercial use up to 1958, when the National Coal Board announced its abandonment in favour of road transport. This was the bi-centenary of Brandling's wagon-way to Leeds, and it was commemorated by a special railtour using open wagons over the remaining 1½ miles to the colliery. In the event, rail access

A near-equivalent to Blenkinsop, Mirvale, *also built by Hudswell Clarke but a year later, on display in the society's Engine House. (Author)*

was kept for the following ten years that the mine operated, but the threat to this historic line led to a Leeds University group forming the Middleton Railway Preservation Society in 1959. The next year there was a ceremonial reopening as part of University Rag Week, when nearly 8,000 passengers travelled free. This was in June, preceding the start of services on the Bluebell Railway in Sussex by two months. In addition, goods trains resumed, serving the industrial premises close to the Leeds end of the line. Over the next ten years, volunteers transformed a derelict and overgrown railway into a line in daily operation and catering both for visitors and freight. There were setbacks: plans to use the former colliery buildings had to be abandoned, and the line was consequently shortened by a further ¼ mile. The northern section (disused since 1948) disappeared in the construction of the M621 motorway in 1971, and one by one the industrial users were lost.

Ex-Manchester Ship Canal no 67 0–6–0ST loco brings the first passenger train of the day back into Moor Road station on a summer Sunday in 2006. (Author)

Now the line survives as a passenger-only preserved railway, operating 1¼ miles of track with plans to extend further into Middleton Park. It was closed for twelve months in 2005–6 for a major redevelopment of its Moor Road headquarters, using a grant from the Heritage Lottery Fund. After reopening at Easter 2006, the railway now has a new station, with shop, café, resource centre and classroom, and a splendid enclosed area for its engines on display. In the summer of that year the society had around fourteen steam locos on site and eleven diesels, with services hauled by diesels on Saturdays and by steam on Sundays. Almost unique in its setting within a large city, the Middleton Railway continues to be a small but successful contributor to the British preservation scene.

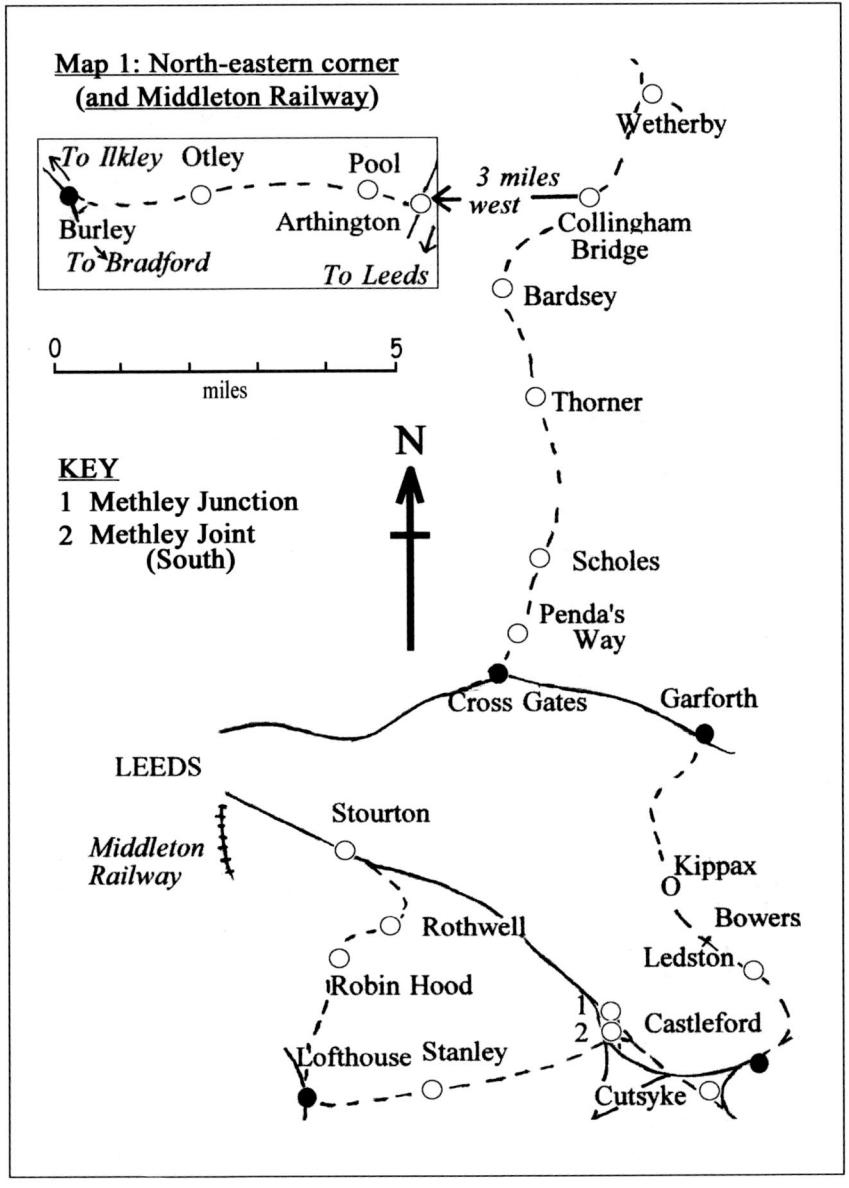

Map 1: North-eastern corner
(and Middleton Railway)

To Ilkley Otley   Pool
Burley   Arthington
To Bradford   To Leeds

3 miles
west   Collingham
            Bridge

Wetherby

Bardsey

Thorner

0   5
        miles

KEY
1 Methley Junction
2 Methley Joint
   (South)

N

Scholes

Penda's
Way

Cross Gates   Garforth

LEEDS

Middleton
Railway

Stourton

Rothwell

Robin Hood

Lofthouse Stanley

Kippax

Bowers

Ledston

1
2   Castleford

Cutsyke

2
North-Eastern Corner

Arthington–Otley–Burley/Cross Gates–Wetherby/
The Ledston Branch/The East & West Yorkshire
Union Railway/The Methley Joint Railway

Ex-NER class R 4–4–0, seen here as LNER no 2342 with a passenger train at Wetherby in the late 1940s. (Author's collection)

Arthington–Otley–Burley

The title 'North-Eastern Corner' for this chapter refers to the area shown in Map 1, rather than the North Eastern Railway (NER), which played a comparatively minor role in South and West Yorkshire, especially considering its dominance in other parts of the county. This area has five closed branches, with varying degrees of NER participation. The first of these to provide passenger services was the line through Otley, a small

An early 20th century view of Otley station, looking east. (Author's collection)

market town in Lower Wharfedale, six miles down-valley from Ilkley.

In the 1850s both the Midland at Skipton, and the NER from its Leeds–Harrogate line, considered expanding into Wharfedale. Agreement was reached in 1860 whereby the Midland would build a line into Ilkley from the west, while the NER would reach Otley from the east. The Ilkley–Otley link would be jointly built, owned and run by the two companies. Surprisingly, both the joint construction and that of the NER opened in 1865. However, the NER was first into Otley, running its trains from Arthington on the Leeds–Harrogate line on 1st February, with the Midland following on 1st August.

On the section of line now closed, a 'Joint' station was provided at Otley, while the NER built stations at Pool (Pool-in-Wharfedale from 1927) and Arthington, which was relocated from its original position on the Leeds–Harrogate line to better serve the branch. The involvement of the two companies meant that initially Otley was well served by Midland trains from both Leeds and Bradford, via Guiseley, and NER services from Leeds

17

LNER Sentinel railcar no 2133 Cleveland *operated on the Leeds–Otley–Ilkley passenger service in the 1930s (also from Wetherby). (Author's collection)*

via Arthington. In 1876 the Midland opened a Shipley–Guiseley cut-off via Baildon, which simplified serving the area from Bradford. However, it was the NER that took most advantage of this, starting a Bradford–Harrogate service via Otley the following year. By 1910 there were nine weekday trains each way, more than either the Midland (five) or NER (six) were running to Otley as a destination.

The Midland services to Otley appear to have ended with the Grouping of 1923, leaving the newly formed LNER to continue the Bradford–Harrogate and Leeds–Otley trains, the latter usually continuing on to Ilkley. The Harrogate service even included a private subscription club car, described as 'an ancient six-wheel saloon with toilet, bathroom and cocktail cabinet'! More prosaically the Leeds service was often handled by Sentinel steam railcars. The services were severely cut back

18

Preserved LNER class K4 2–6–0 no 3442 The Great Marquess *with a railtour at Otley in 1963, two years before the station closed. (Author's collection)*

in the Second World War, but Otley station kept busy with wood pulp trains for the local paper mills and troop trains for the nearby Army camp at Farnley. Otley station's most distinguished visitor was possibly Winston Churchill, who visited the camp on 31st March 1944, and was then driven through the town in an open-top car before catching his special train, with a military band giving him a musical send-off.

The local services did not recover after the war. First to go were the Bradford–Harrogate trains, down to only one a day from 1950 and ending completely in 1957, although there was a brief revival in the summer of 1960 with a service of eleven Sunday DMUs between Bradford and Knaresborough. The Leeds trains were down to four on weekdays by 1957 and three after dieselisation two years later. These continued up to 1965, when the service became a 'Beeching' casualty, with few protests, unlike the Ilkley section where a vigorous campaign ensured that 3½ miles of the Joint line remain in use today. The Otley passenger service was withdrawn on 22nd March, with goods ending in July. By then the last passenger train had passed through – a Preston–York excursion on 7th June. Demolition began the following year and now there is little sign of the railway.

Cross Gates–Wetherby

In 1865 the NER was concerned by a proposal for a Leeds–Stockton line from a rival company, and put forward a line from Cross Gates, 4 miles east of Leeds, to Wetherby as part of an alternative. When the Leeds–Stockton scheme was rejected in Parliament, the NER tried to abandon its proposals and only went ahead after local protests. The 10-mile branch from Cross Gates was opened in 1876, and linked the Leeds–Selby line to the Church Fenton–Wetherby line built by the York & North Midland Railway in 1847–8. The junction at Wetherby only faced towards Church Fenton, so the branch was little used for services to Harrogate until the turn of the century. In 1901 the line was doubled, and both a south-to-west curve and a new station were built at Wetherby. This was all part of a scheme to open up the Leeds–Wetherby–Harrogate–Northallerton route for express traffic, despite the Cross Gates–Wetherby line's problems with landslips. In 1877 passengers had to walk round a landslip near Thorner, in 1907 the line was closed for nineteen days and, in 1953, the down line was shut for a further twelve days.

In 1932 there were four Leeds–Wetherby–Harrogate weekday trains (plus five from Wetherby to Harrogate), with twelve local stopping trains to Wetherby, most continuing to Tadcaster and Church Fenton. Stations had been provided at Scholes, Thorner (originally called Scarcroft), Bardsey and Collingham Bridge, where the River Wharfe was crossed on a 90 ft two-span bridge. In 1939 a new station was added at Penda's Way, under a mile from Cross Gates, to serve a large Leeds housing estate. The site had been cleared and foundations laid previously, but the actual

20

Ex-LMS class 4F 0–6–0 no 44467 with a railtour through Wetherby in 1963. (P. Wilson)

Wetherby station building in 1970, six years after closure to passengers but before its eventual demolition. (Author's collection)

construction took a mere twenty hours. In that time two 120-yard platforms, station buildings and a footbridge were built and painted. On 5th June the station opened, with the first ticket ceremoniously issued to the Lord Mayor of Leeds. Cross Gates–Penda's Way was a popular trip for youngsters in the 1940s, when the child's return fare was only one penny.

Under BR the local passenger traffic went into decline, despite dieselisation of some services in 1958. By the end of 1963 the Leeds–Wetherby trains were down to four on weekdays, plus an extra on Saturdays. Strangely enough the long-distance passenger services had been increased at this time, with three overnight trains transferred to the line in 1959, and two years later two Liverpool–Newcastle expresses each way were added. This was not enough to save the route, which was recommended for closure by Beeching, and it and the

Even after conversion to a pub and restaurant, the former station building at Scholes still shows its NER origins. (Author)

Harrogate–Church Fenton line had the dubious distinction of being the first-ever Beeching closures on 6th January 1964. Goods traffic continued on the Cross Gates–Wetherby line for another four months and the line was then abandoned. Much of the trackbed is intact and can be walked, with the notable exception of the crossing of the Wharfe where the viaduct was demolished. Most of the buildings have also gone, leaving only the former Scholes station building and the station house at Collingham Bridge.

The Ledston branch

Local businessmen and colliery owners in the area north of Castleford commissioned a survey for an independent railway from Garforth to Castleford in 1872. This was opposed by the NER but received the Royal Assent in 1873. However, the finance proved hard to raise and the proposed Leeds, Castleford & Pontefract Junction Railway had to be rescued by the NER after all. That company took over the powers of construction soon after work started in 1875, so that the line's two original

Kippax station in the early years of the 20th century, with its gardens apparently meriting 'First Prize'. (Lens of Sutton Association)

stations at Kippax and Ledstone (after the spelling of a nearby hall, but spelt 'Ledston' from 1915) were built to a typical NER design. The line had probably only been intended for freight, but the NER took the opportunity to introduce a Leeds–Castleford passenger service. This began in 1878 and two years later was extended to Pontefract, using a new connection between Castleford and Cutsyke (which is still in use today).

The line was single-track with no passing places, suggesting its industrial origins. It was quite steeply graded, reaching 1 in 85 in places, and causing difficulties for loaded coal trains. Its main feature was the 900-ft bridge over the Aire, built with eleven spans and room for a second track, which it seems was never laid. The basic weekday passenger service in 1914 was six Leeds–Castleford trains, four of which continued to Pontefract. All trains terminated at Castleford from 1926, but a simple halt, with a single platform only long enough for two coaches, was added at Bowers to serve a nearby housing estate in 1934. The meagre passenger service was reduced to three trains a day by 1949, and was amongst the first in the country to be withdrawn after nationalisation. BR ended the passenger

Ex-LNER class G5 0–4–4T no 67308 with a Leeds–Castleford passenger train at Ledston in 1949. (Author's collection)

trains on 22nd January 1951, with all Castleford services for Leeds then leaving Cutsyke station and travelling via the ex-Methley Joint line.

After closure, there were occasional Sunday diversions of main line expresses to and from Leeds, and a few railtours. Passenger excursions out from the line continued well into the 1960s, trips from Castleford to the coast often beginning at Kippax, where the working men's club sometimes required three separate trains for its seaside outings. Goods traffic kept the line busy, at least at the southern end, with colliery waste coming onto the line for disposal until 1987, and coal shipments out continuing intermittently until 1994. The line was later abandoned, although a mile of rusting track remains at the Castleford end. The bridge over the Aire also survives, in very poor condition. Nothing is left at the station sites, but the trackbed from Kippax north to Garforth has been made into a cycleway.

The East & West Yorkshire Union Railway

Despite the grand title, this was a 5-mile colliery branch which ran a passenger service for a mere nine months, thus only just qualifying for inclusion in this book. It was, however, a genuinely independent line, never part of the NER, and could have featured in a much larger scheme. The Hull & Barnsley Railway, dealt with in Chapter 9, failed to get running powers for access into Leeds. Instead, in 1883, it promoted the East & West Yorkshire Union Railway (E&WYUR) to run from its own main line at Drax for eighteen miles to the Great Northern Railway (GNR) at Ardsley, with a 5-mile extension to Rothwell in a coal-mining district controlled by the Charlesworth family. The Bill was passed at the second attempt in 1883, but the finance needed for such an ambitious scheme was never forthcoming. By 1886 the plan for a line towards Hull had been abandoned, but the

Rothwell Haigh Colliery early in the 20th century. This was one of the pits owned by the Charlesworths who promoted the E&WYUR. (Author's collection)

26

Charlesworths continued with a version of the Rothwell branch to at least get their coal out via the GNR at Lofthouse. In 1892 they formed the nominally separate South Leeds Junction Railway (SLJR) to extend the branch to Leeds. This scheme was rejected in 1892, but a shortened version to the Midland at Stourton was accepted the following year. The E&WYUR had opened for goods traffic in 1891, followed by the SLJR four years later, with the two companies amalgamating in 1896.

The original 1883 proposals had included a Hull–Leeds passenger service, for which feeder trains from Rothwell might well have been feasible. However, the provision 21 years later of a separate passenger service on the E&WYUR made little sense. Horse-drawn wagonettes already ran to Leeds, and a scheme for electric trams to Wakefield had been approved in 1902. A junction with the Midland main line at Stourton had to be built, the SLJR section of track doubled, modern signalling installed,

Little remains of the E&WYUR except for this bridge carrying the A61 at Robin Hood, with the former line now used for a footpath. (Author)

The line was visited in 1958 by this railtour headed by ex-LNER class J6 0–6–0 locos 64222 and 64268, seen here at Rothwell. (J. Davenport)

and platforms built at the three stations of Robin Hood, Rothwell and Stourton. Despite the cost, the E&WYUR went ahead and on 4th January 1904, using carriages hired from the Midland, passenger trains ran from Robin Hood to Wellington Street station in Leeds. There was a basic daily service of five weekday trains each way, with an extra on Tuesdays and Saturdays and three on Sundays.

The station at Stourton was only small, with short platforms and no shelters, but the other two were more substantial, especially Rothwell which had the offices for the company and its executives. Whatever the facilities, the passenger service was not a success, the Sunday service ending after only eight months. In August 1904 the Wakefield electric tramway opened through Lofthouse and Robin Hood. While through tramway services to Leeds did not begin until 1905, the threat seems to have been enough for the E&WYUR, which withdrew its passenger services on 30th September 1904. The company then concentrated on freight, especially coal shipments. Stourton station was demolished by 1919 but the other two continued in use as goods depots.

In 1923 the line became part of the LNER and passenger workings were resumed, though only for excursions. Bridlington and Cleethorpes were the usual destinations, with Blackpool added after 1947. In the late 1950s and early 1960s, Mrs Cotton, the wife of Rothwell's stationmaster, organised trips to Blackpool and Scarborough, even after the couple moved to Stanningley. Railtours also ventured on the branch at this time, but in 1961 the line was severed and closed completely five years later. Today there is almost nothing to be seen of it except for a short walkable stretch at Robin Hood.

The Methley Joint Railway

This line counts as 'north-eastern' by location and 'North Eastern' from that company's share in the joint ownership with the LYR and GNR. However, this was very much the latter's project, as it promoted the original scheme in 1863, with the LYR

A typical coalfield scene with ex-LNER class 01 2–8–0 no 63823 at Methley Junction in 1960. (Author's collection)

Stanley station in 1963, a year before closure to passengers. (Author's collection)

The former Methley South station building is still largely intact. (Author)

and NER admitted as partners after first objecting. The 5-mile Joint line ran eastwards from a triangular junction with the GNR at Lofthouse through a station at Stanley to one at Methley, called Methley South by BR from 1951. This was to distinguish it from the station on the North Midland line to Leeds (Methley North from 1950) and Methley Junction station on the LYR route through Cutsyke to Pontefract and Knottingley. The latter line had opened in 1849 in time for GNR Leeds–Doncaster trains to the St Leger race meeting, via the Askern branch (see Chapter 5). It was one of two lines reached by short spurs from Methley's Joint station, the other being the NER line through Castleford.

The Methley Joint opened for goods in 1865, but it was another four years before the first passenger services. These were GNR services from Castleford Central station on the NER line, to Leeds and to Wakefield. Although the LYR connection was provided with platforms at Methley's Joint station, these were never used as the LYR concentrated on freight, especially coal, at this location. By 1914 the GNR was running nine Leeds–Castleford weekday trains on this route, with three extra trains on Saturdays and five Sunday trains. There were two Wakefield–Castleford weekday trains and just one on Sundays. In 1951 there were a similar number of weekday trains between Leeds and Castleford, but no Sunday services, and Wakefield could only be reached by changing at Ardsley. Later in the decade, DMUs were introduced, with an hourly summer Sundays service in 1957 from Castleford through Leeds to Otley and Ilkley. The next year DMUs took over most of the regular Leeds–Castleford services, with 21 weekday trains each way on the Methley Joint line.

However, Methley's Joint station, now Methley South, closed in 1960 and the Beeching Report saw the line as duplicating the direct (former Midland) route to Leeds for passengers from Castleford. Thus in November 1964 the Joint line closed to passenger traffic, along with Stanley station. Trains instead ran through the former Methley Junction station (closed 1943) to Cutsyke, which now became the station for Castleford. However, in 1968, BR reinstated the former NER link into Castleford Central (though the line east from Castleford closed to passengers in 1970), and shut the line through Cutsyke. Part of the Methley Joint line was kept for colliery traffic until 1982 when it was finally closed. Now little of the route can be seen apart from sections of low embankment above the River Calder.

3
Rural Branch to Major Preserved Line

The Keighley & Worth Valley Railway

The tiny station at Damems, photographed in the early years of the 20th century. (Author's collection)

Like many of the branches in Chapter 6, this line at least partly originated from a much grander project. In 1845 a Manchester, Hebden Bridge & Keighley Junction Railway was proposed, including a section along the Worth valley, south of Keighley. Like so many schemes of that period of 'Railway Mania', this came to nothing, but the Worth valley inhabitants pursued the

The more substantial station at Oakworth at a similar date (its restored version was used in the film The Railway Children*). (Author's collection)*

idea. In October 1861 a deputation of locals went to the Midland Railway at Derby, where it was agreed that if a local company (set up later that year as the Keighley & Worth Valley Railway Company) built a line within the valley, the Midland would operate it. An Act was passed in 1862 and work began two years later, although it was 15th April 1867 before the 4¾-mile line opened to the public after a delay of many months due to the washing away of 40 yards of embankment near Damems. Other problems included the rebuilding of a Methodist chapel undermined by the construction of a 150-yard tunnel at Ingrow. These difficulties had helped push the cost of building the line to over three times the original estimate of £36,000. The first train comprised seven coaches for invited guests, who adjourned for dinner at the Mechanics' Institute, Haworth (a last-minute replacement for Branwell Brontë's local hostelry, the Black Bull). The same day public services began with a timetable of six trains on weekdays and two on Sundays.

Stations were provided at Ingrow, Damems (from September 1867), Oakworth, Haworth and Oxenhope on the single-track route, although enough land had been purchased for doubling. In 1881 the Midland bought the line; by 1910 services had increased to sixteen to eighteen weekday trains and seven on Sundays. The Sunday service ended in 1947, and Damems station closed two years later. In 1959 BR applied to close the branch but was refused and, in June 1960, a full DMU service was introduced of eight weekday trains, with five extra on Saturdays. However, BR applied again to close the line the next year, this time successfully, and the last regular passenger train left Keighley at 11.15 pm on 30th December 1961, with around 150 passengers. Goods services lasted another six months, by which time moves to preserve the line were under way.

In March 1962 the Keighley & Worth Valley Railway Preservation Society was formed and, following the example of the Bluebell Railway in Sussex, attempted to lease the line. BR, however, insisted on selling the line and after complex negotiations this was agreed in September 1964. After many delays, passenger services resumed at last on 29th June 1968, with USA 0–6–0T no 30078 and ex-BR 2–6–2T 41241. Initial services were seven trains on Saturdays and Bank Holidays and six on Sundays, but these proved so popular that they were increased from the end of August to nine and seven. Midweek summer services began the next year, and passenger numbers were greatly increased by the release of the film *The Railway Children* in 1970. By 1975 it was estimated that yearly passenger numbers exceeded those in BR's final year, 1961. Today the line continues the pattern of weekend trains throughout the year, with daily services in July and August, in school holiday weeks in February, May and October, and at Easter, Whitsun and Christmas. As many as eleven trains each way run at summer weekends, taking 25 minutes for the 330-ft climb to Oxenhope, with gradients as steep as 1 in 58 on the sharp curve out of Keighley station. The line is now back to its full complement of stations with Oakworth, Haworth and Oxenhope essentially the original buildings. Ingrow, however, is a replacement, while

A late BR steam scene with class 2MT 2–6–2T no 41326 heading over Mytholmes Viaduct, built as part of an 1892 deviation to avoid a lengthy wooden trestle viaduct. (P. Wilson)

Damems also lost its original building and now has a former checkers' hut from Keighley goods yard!

Over 30 locomotives are now based at the railway, both steam and diesel. Five steam engines comprise the current service fleet, including ones from the Taff Vale, the LMS and BR, also ex-Lancashire & Yorkshire 0–6–0 no 957, which featured in *The Railway Children* film as 'The Green Dragon'. Diesel locos are in use at Haworth and Oxenhope yards, with DMUs in particular available for service. There are also 'guest appearances' by visiting locos, for instance ex-LMS Jubilee class 4–6–0 no 5690 *Leander* at 2006's Autumn Gala. The line has become well known through its use in films, including *Yanks* in 1978, as well as the ever-popular *Railway Children*, and TV series such as *Poirot* and *A Touch of Frost*. Helped by its fine scenery and the Brontë connection at Haworth, the line remains one of the country's top railway-based tourist attractions.

An age gone by is well captured in this approach to the K&WVR platform at Keighley. (Author)

A present-day scene at Haworth with ex-BR class 4MT 2–6–4T no 80002 on a train for Oxenhope at Easter 2006. (Author)

4
Lost Empire – the Great Northern Railway

Direct line to Bradford/The GNR through Batley and Dewsbury/Pudsey/Laisterdyke–Shipley/ The Queensbury lines

Beeston Junction in 1953 with ex-LNER class A1 4-6-2 no 60130 Kestrel *on the 'Queen of Scots' Pullman, and the lines to and from Batley at the extreme left and right. (C. Ord collection)*

Direct line to Bradford

The Great Northern Railway (GNR) reached this area in 1848 at Askern Junction, four miles north of Doncaster (see Chapter 5). Over the next 45 years the company built or acquired another

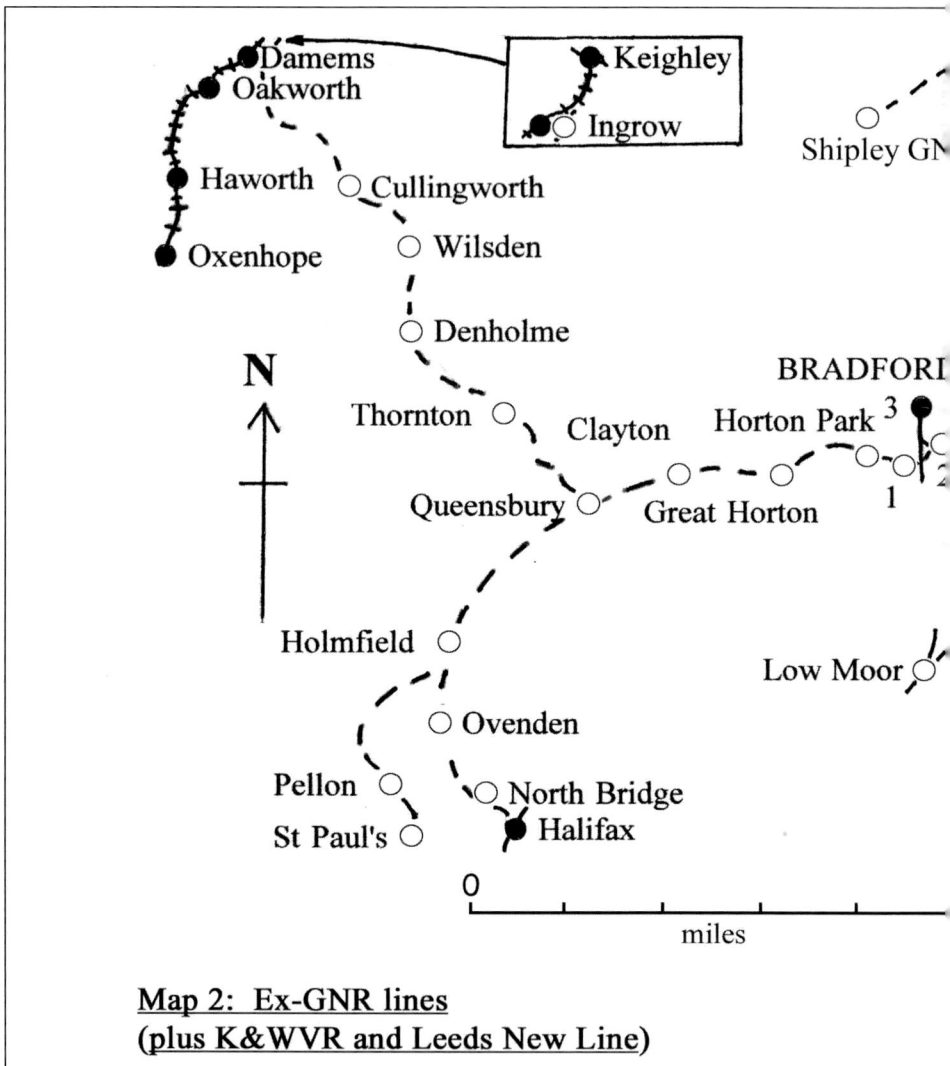

Map 2: Ex-GNR lines
(plus K&WVR and Leeds New Line)

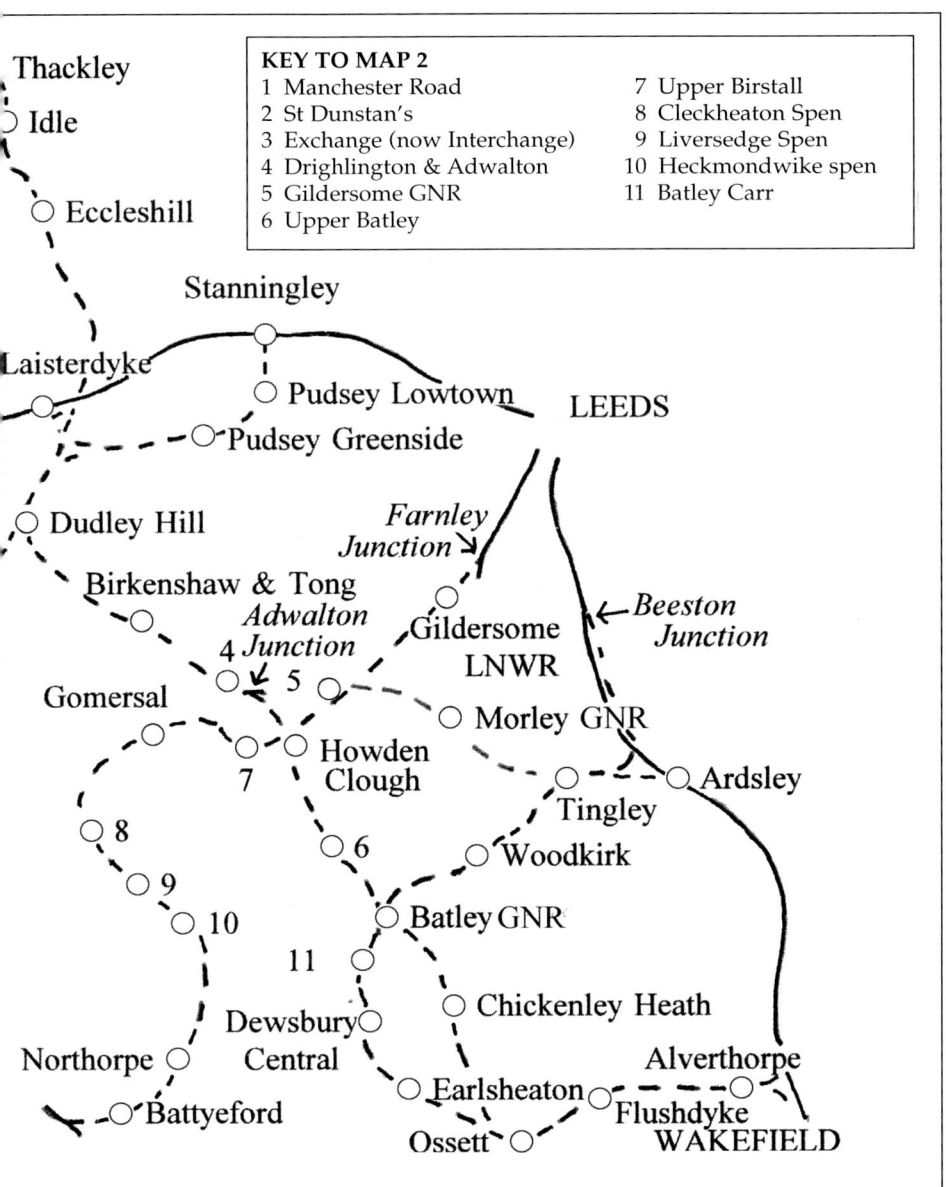

KEY TO MAP 2

1 Manchester Road
2 St Dunstan's
3 Exchange (now Interchange)
4 Drighlington & Adwalton
5 Gildersome GNR
6 Upper Batley
7 Upper Birstall
8 Cleckheaton Spen
9 Liversedge Spen
10 Heckmondwike spen
11 Batley Carr

Thackley
Idle
Eccleshill
Stanningley
Laisterdyke
Pudsey Lowtown
LEEDS
Pudsey Greenside
Dudley Hill
Farnley Junction
Birkenshaw & Tong
Adwalton Junction
Gildersome LNWR
Beeston Junction
Gomersal
Morley GNR
Howden Clough
Ardsley
Tingley
Woodkirk
Batley GNR
Chickenley Heath
Dewsbury Central
Northorpe
Earlsheaton
Alverthorpe
Battyeford
Ossett
Flushdyke
WAKEFIELD

115 miles of passenger lines in Yorkshire, reaching as far west as Halifax and Keighley; 75 miles of these had lost their passenger services by 1966, leaving only the Doncaster–Wakefield–Leeds–Bradford main line still in use today. Among the losses was the direct line from Wakefield to Bradford, bypassing Leeds.

As with many schemes, this was built by a nominally independent company, later absorbed by the GNR. First was the 'Gildersome coal branch', six miles of line built by the Leeds, Bradford & Halifax Junction Railway (LB&HJR) south and east from Laisterdyke on the same company's Leeds–Bradford line. In August 1856 it opened for passengers as well as coal, with a directors' train of 100 passengers out for a 'jaunt' along the line on the 19th, and public services the next day. Stations were built at Dudley Hill, Birkenshaw & Tong, Drighlington & Adwalton and Gildersome, still some eight miles from Wakefield. As early as 1854, however, the potential for a through line had been realised, and the LB&HJR applied for an extension through a station at Morley (called Morley Top from 1951) to Ardsley on the Leeds–Wakefield line. The Gildersome–Ardsley section opened in October 1857, with surprisingly low-key celebrations and, in December, the first Bradford–London King's Cross (via Morley) express service was introduced. For a short spell, 1859–63, the LB&HJR handled the line's local services, but in 1865 it was finally taken over by the GNR.

In 1859 the Gildersome–Ardsley section gained a new intermediate station at Tingley, but five years later it began to lose local traffic to a line completed from Batley to Adwalton Junction, between the stations at Drighlington and Gildersome. By 1922 most of the eastern section's fifteen Monday–Friday local trains were stopping services from Lofthouse and Wakefield to Drighlington, where they connected with the sixteen faster Wakefield–Batley–Bradford trains over the western section. The London–Bradford expresses, however, favoured the Morley route, with three on weekdays, as against one via Batley.

This pattern continued up to the 1950s, with increased traffic at holiday times: for example, a July 1939 LNER evening

Up to dieselisation in the 1950s, most local services were hauled by ex-GNR locos such as this 0–6–0 engine, seen here as LNER class J6 no 4226. (Author's collection)

excursion to Scarborough, which cost 2s 8d for a third class return. In the 1950s and 60s the line's passenger facilities seem to have just withered away; Dudley Hill was the first closure in 1952, followed by Birkenshaw & Tong in 1953, Tingley in 1954 and Gildersome in 1955. With the introduction of DMUs in 1957, the Wakefield–Batley–Bradford service was up to seventeen trains on weekdays, but local stopping services through Morley were withdrawn, leaving the line's eastern section with only three Monday–Friday trains connecting with London expressses at Wakefield. Station closures continued with Morley in 1961, and Drighlington & Adwalton the next year. The Wakefield–Batley–Bradford service was a Beeching casualty in 1964, and the last remaining London connection through Morley ended in 1966. That year the line had been busy with diversions due to the construction of New Pudsey station on the

The simple station at Tingley in 1956, two years after closure to passengers. (D. Thompson)

Morley's GNR station has gone but the former goods shed survives, though in use for a different form of transport! (Author)

Leeds–Bradford line, but by the end of October its central section had closed altogether. The rest of the line closed in stages, ending with Laisterdyke–Dudley Hill in 1981 (the last ex-GNR line closure in West Yorkshire), and now very little remains to show that a railway ever existed here. Careful research reveals a few remnants, for example, Morley's former goods depot and stationmaster's house (appropriately located at the end of Great Northern Street).

The GNR through Batley and Dewsbury

In the early 1860s the two nominally independent companies that had provided the GNR with its access to Leeds and Bradford were also involved in schemes for lines to the growing mill town of Batley. The Bradford, Wakefield & Leeds Railway (BW&LR), which had opened the Wakefield–Leeds line in 1857, began construction at the Wakefield end, reaching Ossett in April 1864 and Batley eight months later. Meanwhile the LB&HJR, which had built the direct line through Adwalton in 1856–7, began extending south from there, to Upper Batley in 1863 and Batley the following year. Thus, by the time the GNR

Adwalton Junction was the northern end of this line, seen here with ex-GNR class N1 0–6–2T no 69474. (Author's collection)

Reminders of the GNR at Dewsbury – the Station Hotel with beyond it the frontage of the former Central station. (Author)

absorbed both companies in 1865, it had an alternative through route to Bradford via Batley.

The new line initially had stations at Flushdyke, Ossett, Batley (where the GNR had its own platforms at the station originally built by the LNWR in 1848) and Upper Batley. Howden Clough was added in 1866, Alverthorpe six years later and Chickenley Heath in 1877. By then the GNR was building a loop through Dewsbury, reaching the town from Ossett in 1874, and completing the route six years later. Again stations were added piecemeal; Earlsheaton opened in 1875 and Batley Carr in 1880, along with Dewsbury Central, which replaced the temporary 1874 terminus. The final piece in the jigsaw was a heavily engineered extension north from Batley, through Tingley on the direct line to Bradford, to Beeston Junction on the 1857 line to Leeds. This opened in 1890, with a single additional station at Woodkirk.

46

Ex-LNER class J50 0–6–0T no 68904 at Batley's GNR platforms in 1963. (Author's collection)

By the early 20th century there was a variety of services over these lines. The most important were from Bradford to Batley, Dewsbury and Wakefield, with as many as 30 weekday trains each way (6 on Sundays) plus a couple of London expresses. The original route from Ossett to Batley had been relegated to a branch line, served by a sparse railmotor service nicknamed the 'Chickenley Coddy', though even this ended in 1909. The Batley–Tingley–Beeston route had some interesting workings, including an LYR service from Barnsley to Leeds, which lingered on until 1923, although the more usual workings north of Tingley were trains on a roundabout route from Bradford. In 1890 the GNR introduced a Leeds–Ardsley–Dewsbury–Batley–Tingley–Leeds circuit, with three weekday trains each way, which lasted until 1939. A second route followed in 1893; this was a joint GNR/LYR venture linking Leeds with Tingley,

Batley, Dewsbury, the LYR Spen Valley line, Low Moor and Pudsey before returning to Leeds, but this ended in 1914.

There was a long period of local station closures starting with Woodkirk in 1939, followed by Flushdyke (1941), Batley Carr (1950), Upper Batley and Howden Clough (1952), Earlsheaton (1953) and Alverthorpe (1954). The first line closure was the Batley–Tingley–Beeston section, in 1951 to passengers and for goods two years later, but Dewsbury and Batley continued to be served by Bradford–Wakefield trains, with seventeen weekday DMUs from 1957. However, the line was nominated for closure in the Beeching Report, and passenger services were withdrawn on 7th September 1964. Now very little remains, and most of these lines have disappeared completely. Surprisingly the Batley–Beeston section has the most remnants, with the sealed-off 658-yard Soothill Tunnel, ruins of the station buildings at Woodkirk, and a fine viaduct over the main line to Leeds south of Beeston.

Pudsey

The thriving manufacturing town of Pudsey, with a population of almost 15,000 in the 1870s, had protested since 1856 at the lack of a rail link. Eventually in 1877 the GNR opened a single-track branch into the town from Stanningley on its Leeds–Bradford line, allowing a passenger service from Bradford to Pudsey Lowtown and Pudsey Greenside to begin the next year. The line was later doubled and a curve was added in 1893 for access from Leeds, plus a connection west to the Bradford direct line between Dudley Hill and Laisterdyke. These converted the branch into a through route, and a further connection south towards Dudley Hill, plus a 2-mile branch from there to Low Moor, also opened in 1893. They made possible the second GNR circuit described earlier, which only lasted until 1914, with the Dudley Hill–Low Moor branch closing completely three years later. In 1938 the connection from the Pudsey loop to Dudley Hill closed to passenger traffic, leaving the town with only services west to Bradford and east to

Greenside, seen here in 1963, was the more important of the two Pudsey stations. (Stations UK)

Leeds. Even in 1946 on weekdays there were twenty passenger trains each way using the loop, but in 1961 the number was down to ten although the service was now dieselised. The route was seen by Beeching as unnecessary duplication, and the line and Pudsey's two stations closed to passengers on 15th June 1964. The end for goods came three weeks later, with demolition of the stations the following year. Now little is left except the sealed-off Greenside Tunnel and the Smalewell embankment, reputedly the highest in Europe.

Pudsey resident Mick Coulson began working on the railways at the age of 14 as an oiler and greaser at Leeds Central station. He progressed to work as a fireman at the former GNR Copley Hill shed and, as a fireman, worked on the Leeds–Bradford lines through both Pudsey (now closed) and Stanningley (still open). At this time, post-Second World War, the Pudsey line handled most of the Leeds–Bradford local traffic, and saw a regular passenger service from 5 am till late at night. The Pudsey stations were busiest in the town's August holidays, with seaside specials to the Yorkshire coast. Of the two, he considered Greenside the more important station, especially for freight, as there were small sidings specifically for coal deliveries. As a postscript, Mick remembered his last day on BR's Eastern Region in 1962, as driver on the 'Queen of Scots' Pullman non-stop from King's Cross to Leeds – the service shown in this chapter's opening photograph.

Laisterdyke–Shipley

This GNR branch to Shipley, three miles north of Bradford, was unusual in that two separate companies were originally involved in its construction. The Bradford, Eccleshill & Idle Railway was incorporated in 1866, and the Idle & Shipley Railway the following year, but even with GNR backing neither could raise the capital needed and so the GNR took over in 1871. Four years later, the 6¼-mile double-track line was completed with capacious stations at Eccleshill, Idle and Shipley (GNR), the latter also confusingly known as Shipley & Windhill and Shipley Bridge Street at various times. A further station was added at Thackley in 1878. A suburban passenger service to and from Bradford was attempted, but this was not a success. The station at Shipley was further from the town centre than its Midland rival (which is still open today), and journey times to Bradford were longer. The Midland opposed GNR trains using its Shipley station, and ruled out any kind of circular route. Freight was always more important with coal and limestone coming on to the branch, and building stone sent out from quarries at Idle.

By 1922 there were still ten weekday passenger trains both ways, but the LNER soon ended the service. Passenger trains were withdrawn on 2nd February 1931, and the line reduced to a single track for freight only for well over 30 more years. Occasional passenger excursions and railtours did continue into the 1960s. As late as 1964, the line was still being used for

A rare view of passenger services at Shipley & Windhill, with ex-GNR 4–4–2T no 4549. (Lens of Sutton Association)

The station building has been well preserved and is used by several businesses. (Author)

express freight services from Bradford to Manchester, but that year the line was closed south of Idle. The Shipley end stayed in use for goods for another four years before final closure. Most of the line's route has been lost to Bradford's expansion, and the only significant remnants are the former station buildings at Shipley and Thackley (now a residence).

The Queensbury lines

The land between Bradford, Halifax and Keighley rises to over 1300 ft above sea level, and is split by deep valleys. Between 1864 and 1890, the GNR spent over £1 million on a rail network for this area, all of it closed by 1974. With a total of sixteen tunnels, four major viaducts and several grades as steep as 1 in 50, the lines were an extraordinary engineering achievement, and so difficult to work that they were named the 'Alpine Route' by engine crews.

A bird's eye view of the famous triangular platform layout at Queensbury, seen from the Halifax direction with lines to Keighley and Bradford heading left and right respectively. (Author's collection)

Wilsden station exterior in pre-Grouping days. (Lens of Sutton Association)

Only the station cottages remain from the earlier scene, along with the road bridge over the former trackbed. (Author)

The network began with a scheme for a three-mile section north from Halifax promoted by the Halifax & Ovenden Junction Railway in 1864. Both the GNR and LYR subscribed to the venture and jointly took over the project in 1870. By this time the difficulties of railway construction through this kind of terrain were all too apparent. The first problem was the need for a 480-yard viaduct between Halifax and the next station, North Bridge, which involved the clearance of many properties, and then a massive earth slip near North Bridge held up construction for almost a year. Two tunnels and a second viaduct were required before the stations at Ovenden and Holmfield were reached, finally opening for passengers in 1879.

Meanwhile a privately-sponsored scheme to link Bradford and Thornton via Queensbury was taken over by the GNR in 1872, along with a 'Thornton and Keighley' project and a proposed link from Queensbury to Holmfield. By 1873, the GNR was committed to the whole of what became the Queensbury lines. The next year construction began on the Bradford–Thornton section, and on the Queensbury Tunnel on the link south to Holmfield. The tunnel took four years to complete and, at the time of opening in 1878, was at 2,501 yards the longest on the entire GNR system. By August 1877, the Bradford–Thornton section was open for freight to Clayton, but the GNR was suffering the effects of a national 'great depression' and a start on the Thornton–Keighley section was delayed until 1881. Construction on the Bradford–Thornton section continued, including the 1,057 yard Clayton Tunnel, and the magnificent Thornton Viaduct of 20 arches rising up to 120 ft above the valley. Passenger services began in October 1878, calling at stations at Manchester Road (in Bradford), Great Horton, Clayton and Thornton. The next month, a station at St Dunstan's opened, which was particularly used for connections to Bradford–London trains and, in 1880, one at Horton Park, convenient for Bradford Park Avenue football and cricket grounds. Work on Queensbury station had been delayed by the financial crisis, and it opened in 1879, with only bare platforms and a footpath from the town 400 ft higher up! In 1890 the GNR built a road and opened a 'proper' station, with platforms on all three sides of a triangle; it and Ambergate in Derbyshire were the only examples of this in Britain.

Work on the Thornton–Keighley section proved exceptionally difficult and this section alone cost £282,000. Eight tunnels were required, including the 1,533-yard Lees Moor Tunnel, and two major viaducts at Cullingworth and Hewenden. Passenger services were introduced in stages, Thornton–Denholme in January 1884, on to Cullingworth and Ingrow three months later, and finally to Keighley in November 1884. Another station was added at Wilsden in 1886.

Usually grouped with these lines is the Halifax High Level Railway, opened in 1890 and taken over by the GNR and LYR jointly four years later. This three-mile branch climbed from Holmfield through an intermediate station at Pellon to a terminus at St Paul's, high on the western side of Halifax. In this

The Wheatley Viaduct is one of the few reminders of the Halifax High Level Railway. (Author)

Holmfield station shortly before closure in 1955, with a class N1 loco on a two-coach Halifax train. (Author's collection)

short distance it still required an 819-yard tunnel and a 10-arch viaduct. Services began with ten weekday trains each way, but the line could not compete against the trams introduced early in the 20th century. The passenger service ended in 1917, but the line continued in use for freight until 1960.

Services on the rest of the Queensbury lines had begun in 1878 with seven passenger trains between Bradford and Thornton (four on Sundays), and reached a peak around 1900. A year later, trams reached Queensbury from both Halifax and Bradford, and passenger numbers for the trains began a long slow decline. Manchester Road station closed to passengers in 1915, and Sunday services ended in 1938, but as late as 1946 there were still fifteen Bradford–Halifax weekday trains, nine Bradford–Keighley and twelve Halifax–Keighley, all interconnecting at Queensbury. Under BR, the Halifax–Keighley service virtually ended, and surveys in 1953–4 suggested that closing the Queensbury lines would save £49,000 a year. St Dunstan's and Horton Park had closed to passengers in 1952, and BR announced the withdrawal of all remaining passenger services from 23rd May 1955. Local protests were muted until closure, but there was then considerable pressure for a reinstatement of services, backed by local MPs. All this was to no avail, and the remaining freight services were steadily cut back, finishing with the closure of Horton Park to goods in 1972 and North Bridge two years later.

Today little is left of the trackbed of these lines, although the Great Northern Trail has reopened a one-mile stretch across Cullingworth and Hewenden viaducts as a path for cyclists and walkers, and hopes eventually to complete another four miles of path, mostly on the former line's route, to Queensbury. However, it is the views of the viaducts at Wheatley, Thornton, Cullingworth and Hewenden that best commemorate the incredible endeavour that went into the building of the Queensbury lines.

The splendid seventeen-arch viaduct at Hewenden, now used by the Great Northern Trail. (Author)

5

An Odd Assortment – LNWR and LYR Through Lines

The Pickle Bridge branch/The LYR Spen Valley line/
The Leeds New Line/The Askern branch/
The Dearne Valley Railway

Through working over the Leeds New Line, with ex-LMS Patriot 4–6–0 no 45515 Caernarvon *on a Leeds–Manchester train. (P. Wilson)*

The Pickle Bridge branch

The Yorkshire Calder rises on the western boundary with Lancashire, and flows around 45 miles eastwards to join the Aire at Castleford. In the 19th century, its valley, along with those of its tributaries including the Colne and the Spen, was the railway 'territory' of two companies, the London & North Western Railway (LNWR) and the Lancashire & Yorkshire Railway (LYR). Altogether thirteen of the lines operated by these two companies are now 'lost railways'. Eight minor branches have been left to the next chapter, but five were all through routes of varying importance.

The westernmost of the five is the Pickle Bridge branch, which took its name from the station at its northern end on the Halifax–Bradford line of 1850 (although the station was renamed Wyke in 1882 and relocated fourteen years later). The branch had been sanctioned in 1846 as part of the 45-mile West Riding Union Railway (WRUR) system, but in the following year that company became part of the Manchester-based LYR, whose attitude to Yorkshire railways has been described as 'fickle'. In 1850 the LYR announced it would not build those WRUR lines not yet started, including the Pickle Bridge line.

Bailiff Bridge station in the early years of the 20th century, with a Bradford–Huddersfield local train. (Stations UK)

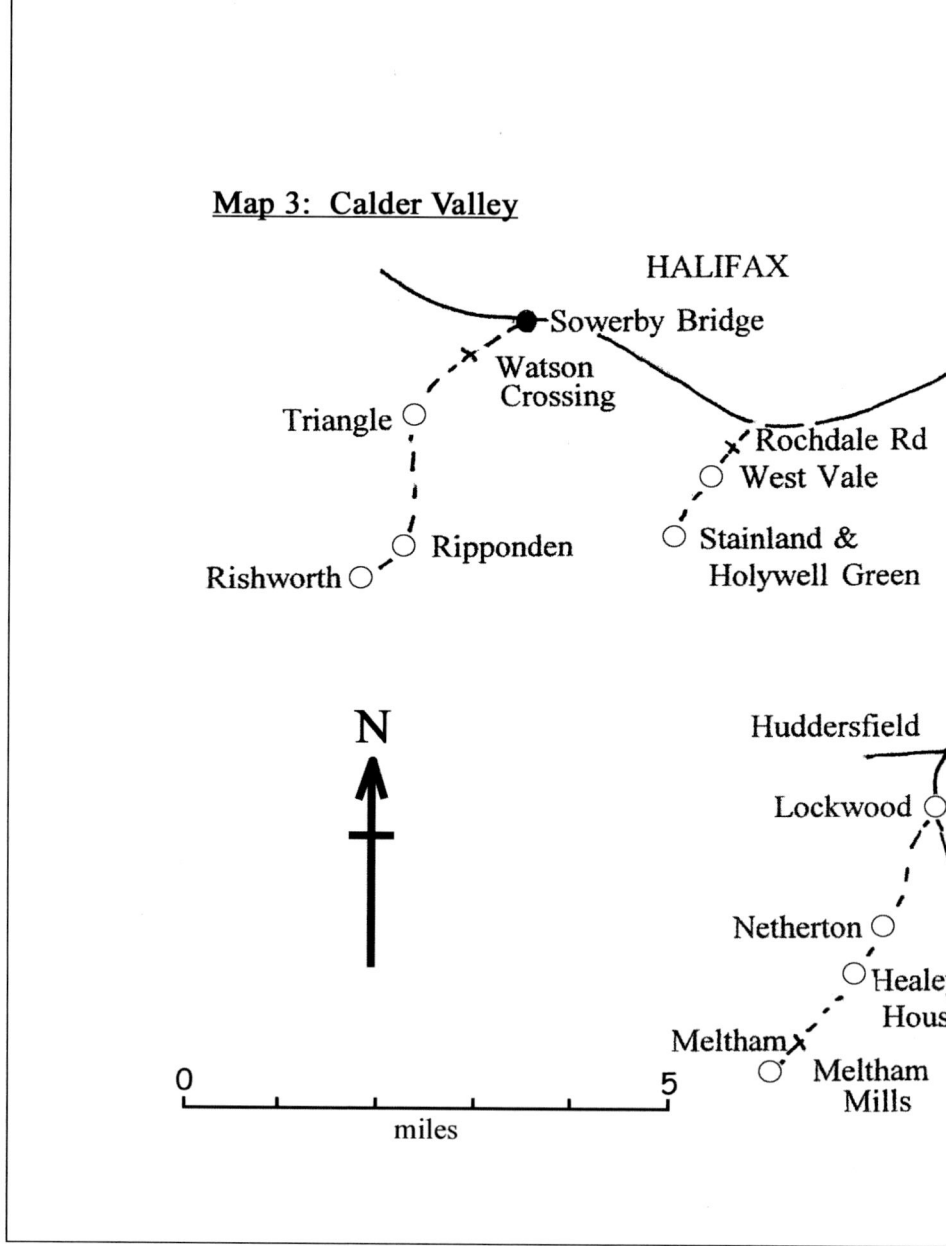

Map 3: Calder Valley

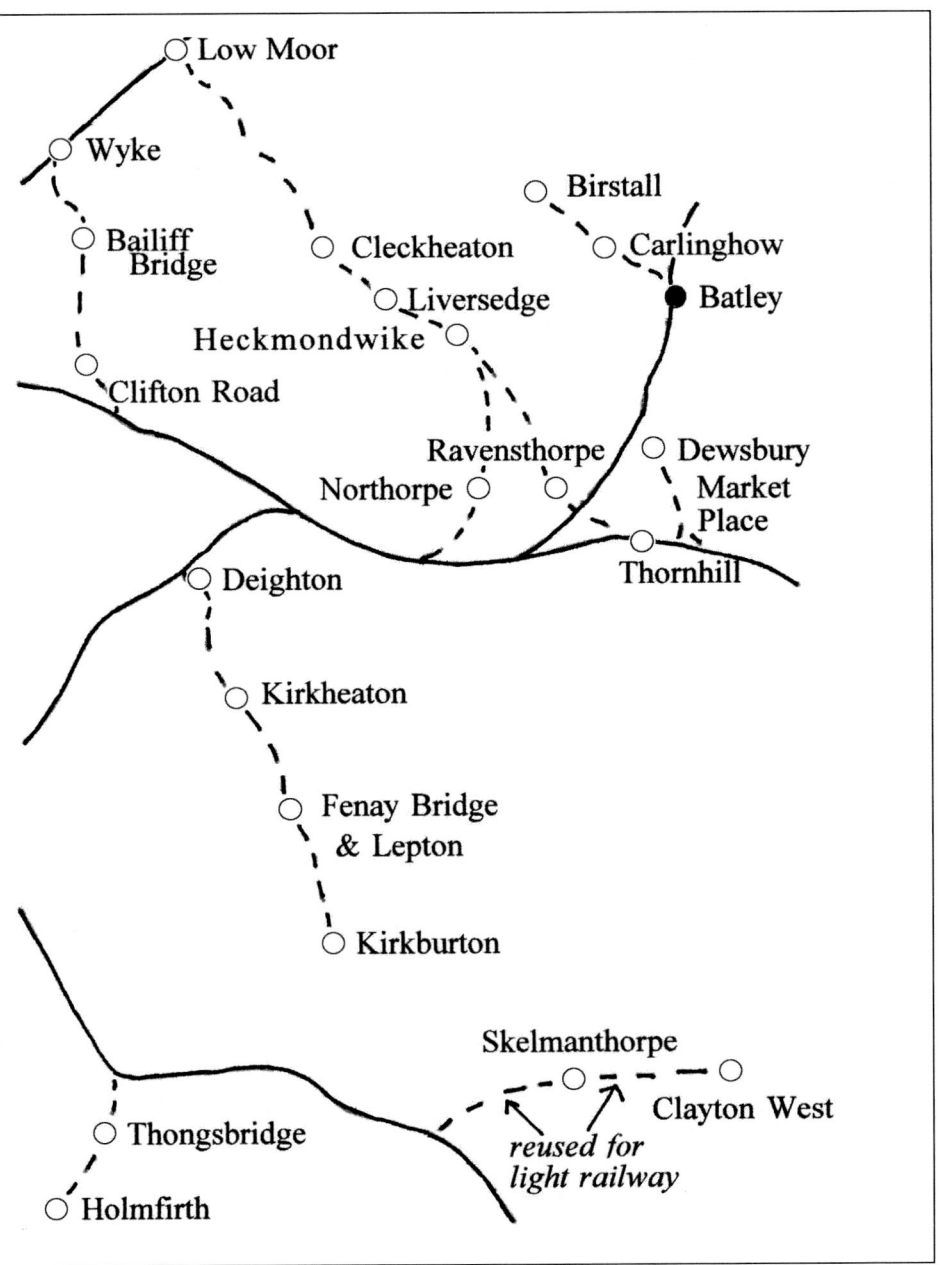

Eventually in 1866, the LYR instead proposed a branch at the northern end as far as Clifton Road, Brighouse, extended seven years later to reach the Calder Valley main line. Another Act was needed in 1875 before the branch finally opened in 1881, 35 years after it was first proposed.

The 3¾-mile branch included two stations at Bailiff Bridge and Clifton Road, but its real importance was for services between Bradford and Huddersfield, including expresses bound for London Marylebone commencing in 1900. By 1910, there were as many as eighteen to twenty weekday passenger trains on the branch, but twelve years later these were down to seven each way, with two London expresses. Bailiff Bridge station closed to passengers in 1917 (and burned down twelve years after), and local services ended altogether in 1931, when Clifton Road also closed. In 1948, the remaining through services were re-routed onto the Spen Valley line, due to

Not a medieval gatehouse but the truncated remains of the Wyke Viaduct, just crossing the A58 Halifax–Leeds road. (Author)

concerns about the state of the 22-arch Wyke Viaduct. Ironically this was a completely unnecessary structure, built only because a local landowner's opposition to the line running over his land forced the line to cross the valley. Now the viaduct that led to the line's early closure is its chief remaining feature – or at least half of it is. Stone blocks falling from its parapet led British Rail to demolish part of it in the 1970s, leaving the other half still straddling the main Halifax–Leeds road.

The LYR Spen Valley line

The Spen is a relatively insignificant tributary, flowing eight miles south-east to join the Calder near Dewsbury, but its valley held two attractions for 19th-century railway builders. It contained the small but growing towns of Cleckheaton, Liversedge and Heckmondwike to provide traffic, but more importantly it was a through route from Bradford to the Calder valley. After the failure of early schemes in 1844–5, a Mirfield–Low Moor line using the valley was part of the WRUR proposals of 1846. This was the first WRUR line to be completed, in 1848, and so preceded the 1850 abandonments. It was formally opened by the LYR on 12th July 1848, when the directors went along the line in a train of 33 carriages hauled by 4 engines, followed by a cold tea in a tent at Cleckheaton. Public services began six days later, but even then the stations at Heckmondwike, Liversedge and Cleckheaton (all of which added 'Central' under the LMS) were not ready. Low Moor remained the terminus until the opening of the Bradford–Halifax line in 1850.

Among the abandoned WRUR projects was a link from Heckmondwike to Thornhill on the Calder Valley main line; the land had been bought, but in 1860 the LYR set up a sub-committee to look into reselling it. Later that year, however, a survey was made and, in 1861, an Act was obtained for this branch, plus those to Dewsbury (Market Place) and Meltham. Even then it was another eight years before the line opened, with a single intermediate station at Ravensthorpe. By 1881, this

Low Moor station, seen here in 1965, was the original terminus for Spen Valley trains. (P.S. Hogg)

later section had around ten weekday trains each way on a Bradford to Wakefield and Normanton service, compared with about a dozen on the original route, generally as part of a Huddersfield–Heckmondwike–Low Moor–Bradford service.

The Spen Valley line gained in importance in 1883 when GNR trains began running over it, and three years later the Low Moor south curve allowed direct access towards Halifax. On the original branch, a further station was added at Northorpe, to which the LMS added 'North Road'. The Spen Valley line became part of the GNR/LYR circuit from Leeds, which started in 1893. After the opening of the GCR's London extension in 1899, it was used by Bradford–London Marylebone expresses hauled by the LYR as far as Sheffield and, by 1914, there were three such trains on weekdays, with one on Sundays. At this time, in addition to the regular LYR trains from Bradford to Dewsbury and Huddersfield, there were GNR excursions to the

Heckmondwike Old Station, in use for passengers from 1848 to 1888, was later relegated to goods duties. (Author's collection)

seaside, NER trains from Halifax to Selby and Hull, and even Midland and Hull & Barnsley special workings. The London expresses continued into the 1920s, when one was indirectly responsible for a bizarre accident at Cleckheaton. On 22nd June 1928, a coal train was being shunted into sidings to make way for the London express. Wagons broke loose, crashed through the buffers, and landed on a butcher's shop in Westgate. Although the shop was flattened, miraculously no one was hurt, although coal dust turned several bystanders 'black as ink'! The event is commemorated with a wall sculpture, plaque and seat at the site.

Services declined under BR, with Ravensthorpe station closing in 1952, followed the next year by the last London expresses as the 'South Yorkshireman' switched to running via Halifax. The Bradford to Dewsbury (latterly to Thornhill) service ended in 1957, leaving the line with only Bradford–Huddersfield local

Liversedge station in LYR days, looking towards Low Moor. (Author's collection)

passenger services. These were dieselised in 1957, but six years later, perhaps surprisingly, the line was suggested for closure to passengers in the Beeching Report. The last passenger trains ran on 12th June 1965, but the Low Moor–Heckmondwike–Thornhill line was retained for freight, even after the construction of the M62 motorway across its route in the early 1970s. A connection to the Leeds New Line at Liversedge allowed access from Thornhill to an oil terminal, which kept part of the line in use until 1986. At Low Moor, the line's northern end was included in an ambitious scheme for a West Yorkshire Transport Museum, which opened in 1995, only to close two years later. Such projects helped preserve the Low Moor–Thornhill section as a through route, available for conversion into the Spen Valley Greenway (cycleway) opened in 2001. The Mirfield–Heckmondwike section has largely been lost, as have most remains of the stations, Cleckheaton's in unusual circumstances. In 1971, while

A curious corner of Cleckheaton commemorating the accident in 1928. (Author)

The Spen Valley Greenway is advertised at the former line's bridge over the A644 at Ravensthorpe. (Author)

awaiting demolition, it completely disappeared overnight. Later that year a man was charged with stealing its stone, timber, metal, railway track and even the buffer stops!

The Leeds New Line

By the 1880s, the main LNWR line between Leeds and Manchester was becoming overloaded with both passenger trains and goods traffic. The company began a programme of quadrupling the track where feasible, and constructing new tunnels, notably the third Standedge tunnel into Lancashire. These improvements left only one 'problem' section within Yorkshire, from Heaton Lodge north-east of Huddersfield to Wortley outside Leeds. The main difficulty was the 3,369-yard Morley Tunnel, which was already suffering subsidence from nearby mining. This ruled out enlarging the tunnel, or even constructing a new bore nearby. The LNWR decided instead to build a completely new railway to allow extra capacity and tap into new areas, particularly the Spen valley towns, which had long been dissatisfied with the service provided by the LYR. This was to be the Heaton Lodge & Wortley Railway, also called the Leeds New Line, shown on Map 2.

Construction of the fourteen-mile line began in 1895, with viaducts at Battyeford and Heckmondwike, and tunnels at Gomersal and Gildersome, the latter 2,339 yards long, as the line climbed 290 ft from both directions to a summit near Birstall. There were also problems in built-up areas, especially Heckmondwike, where 126 houses were bought, demolished, and replaced by 6 blocks of property known locally as the 'Eighty Houses'. The westernmost 2¾ miles were completed first, and opened in September 1899 for goods traffic to stations at Battyeford & Mirfield (Battyeford from 1924) and Northorpe (later Northorpe Higher). The remainder opened for goods in August 1900, and for passengers two months later, services beginning on 1st October with no official ceremony. Stations had been built at the three Spen valley towns of Heckmondwike, Liversedge and Cleckheaton (all of which

Stanier 8F 2–8–0 no 48513 at Battyeford in 1953, shortly before the station closed. (Author's collection)

added 'Spen' in 1924), and further east at Gomersal, Upper Birstal (the historic spelling but changed to Birstall Town from 1935) and Gildersome. The line finished with a 'flying junction' at Farnley, which took westbound trains over the original Leeds–Manchester main line.

The original passenger services of twelve weekday trains each way were all Leeds–Huddersfield stopping trains, with express services kept on the original 1848 main line. Services were later reduced (except on Saturdays), particularly during the First World War. Gildersome station closed from 1917 to 1919, and permanently in 1921 and, in the same year, Northorpe station burnt to the ground. This was a common risk with all-wooden constructions; the same had happened to Heckmondwike goods warehouse in 1915. That was not replaced, but Northorpe station was rebuilt on the other side of its access road. Birstall Town station closed to passengers in

Heckmondwike Old Hall, childhood home of Joseph Priestley and now a pub, was one of many properties in the town affected by the railway (losing its eastern gable). (Author)

1951, and Cleckheaton Spen in January 1953. This station was badly placed, and was only reached from the town centre using a road viaduct, but did reopen for summer holiday trips to Scarborough, Southport and Belle Vue (Manchester). The remaining stations closed with the withdrawal of the local passenger service on 5th October 1953.

The line continued in use for local and through goods workings, and for non-stop passenger trains, including some expresses from Liverpool to Newcastle and Swansea to York. In 1961 'Trans Pennine' DMU services between Hull and Liverpool were added. However, in 1964, all these except one Liverpool–Newcastle train were diverted, this last survivor switching in August 1965, after which the line was closed between Farnley and Liversedge. The connection of the oil terminal at Liversedge to the ex-LYR line allowed the line south

One of the line's few remnants is this road viaduct built for access to Cleckheaton's LNWR station. (Author)

Upper Birstal, later renamed Birstall Town, was an all-wooden construction high on an embankment. (Lens of Sutton Association)

71

of Heckmondwike to close in 1966. The terminal's two-mile link stayed in use until 1986, but now all railway buildings and most of the route have been lost apart from one mile of cycleway through Liversedge, and a sequence of nine bridges within one mile at Heckmondwike.

The Askern branch

This was the LYR's easternmost route, apart from the line to the port of Goole, which it left at Knottingley for the ten miles to Askern Junction (see Map 8). There it made an end-on connection with the GNR, rescuing that company from famously 'ending in a ploughed field four miles north of Doncaster'. The GNR had opened its line north from London King's Cross in 1848–9, but its Doncaster–Leeds scheme was rejected in Parliament. George Hudson, keen to bolster his own railways, offered running powers to the GNR from Knottingley to both Leeds and York. The Askern branch opened in June 1848

A rural scene at Askern station around 1907. (Stations UK)

and was built, like the line to Goole, by the LYR constituent the Wakefield, Pontefract & Goole Railway. Construction had been easy across the level terrain and there were no engineering features, although fifteen level crossings were required.

Thanks to Hudson's scheming, from 1850 to 1871 the route was part of the East Coast Main Line. The opening of the NER Doncaster–Selby–York line ended that role, and, as the line through Askern had already lost the Leeds expresses in 1866, it was left with a Doncaster–Knottingley–Wakefield local service. This comprised seven to eight weekday trains in 1910 (two on Sundays), calling at Askern, Norton and Womersley stations. Some express trains continued to use the line, however, including an LYR Harwich–Liverpool boat train (calling at Askern by request) until 1914, and the 'North Country Continental' to York up to 1939. The GNR and, later LNER, ran King's Cross–Harrogate expresses over the line from 1902 up to

The unusually ornate station building at Womersley, overlooking the track which is still used by freight trains. (Author)

1947, when the local passenger service also ended. Even then the line had regular booked through passenger trains (two each weekday in summer 1955), and diversions from the East Coast Main Line up to the 1990s. Now it only has occasional freight use, chiefly coal trains, but fine station houses survive at Womersley and Norton.

The Dearne Valley Railway

The LYR was not associated, at least in Yorkshire, with many colliery lines, but the Dearne Valley Railway (DVR) was essentially an LYR project. Although the DVR was a nominally independent eighteen-mile line (shown on Map 8), its major officials were shared with the LYR, and its connection north towards Wakefield was built by the LYR, which also provided its rolling stock. When incorporated in 1897, the DVR was linked with the Hull & Barnsley Railway for a direct outlet to Hull, but despite initial running powers for that company, it

This ex-LYR 2–4–2T, seen here at Wakefield as LMS no 10650, worked the line's passenger services in the 1940s. (Author's collection)

74

The last passengers alight from the last train at Goldthorpe Halt in September 1951. (Courtesy of Yorkshire Post Newspapers)

was the LYR that obtained the decisive link-up in 1900. The DVR opened for freight, principally the movement of coal, in stages between 1902 and 1909, with the Junction railway built by the LYR north to Crofton on its Wakefield–Pontefract line opening in 1905. At its other end, the DVR was connected to the GNR system at Black Carr south of Doncaster, thus qualifying as a through line.

However, the line was used as a lengthy branch for its passenger services, which began on 3rd June 1912, and amazingly lasted for almost 40 years. Stations were built that in reality were the most rudimentary halts, with a layer of ash in lieu of a platform, a nameboard, fencing and an old coach body for a 'waiting room'. These meagre facilities were provided at Ryhill on the Junction line, and at Grimethorpe, Great Houghton, Goldthorpe & Thurnscoe, Harlington, Denaby and Edlington on the DVR. Most of these were conveniently sited

This splendid viaduct still crosses the Don valley at Conisbrough. (Author)

for the mining communities, but Denaby halt was intended mainly for the Montague family of nearby Melton Hall. Their demands included the planting of trees to hide the railway from the hall, and an ornamental bridge over the lane, as well as arrangements for use of the halt, which closed in 1949. Passenger trains ran from Wakefield Kirkgate station through the halts to Edlington, an odd choice of terminus three miles from central Doncaster. Initial services were four return runs, operated by one of the LYR's railmotors (see Chapter 6), and taking 55 minutes to cover the route.

A similar service continued, with additional Saturday runs, although the railmotor was replaced first by ex-LYR 2–4–2 tank engines and, latterly, by Ivatt class 2 locos, though still using the coach from the railmotor! It survived the whole LMS era but was an early BR closure, passenger services being withdrawn on 10th September 1951. The line continued in use for freight, especially coal shipments, but a connection was put in to allow these to be taken out via the ex-Midland line in 1966 and the DVR became disused. Today there is little sign that it ever existed, with one magnificent exception. The viaduct over the Don still stands, with its 21 arches and 150-ft lattice girder bridge over the river. One of its claims to fame is that it was built using an aerial ropeway, similar to that used in the construction of the railway bridge over the Zambezi at Victoria Falls! It is certainly the single most impressive feature remaining from the 'lost' railways in this area.

6
Branches Galore – More LNWR and LYR Lines

Rishworth/Stainland/Holmfirth/Meltham/ Clayton West/Kirkburton/Dewsbury (Market Place)/ Birstall

Triangle was one of two small intermediate stops before the larger stations at Ripponden and Rishworth. (Author's collection)

Rishworth

Although all eight of these former LYR/LNWR lines in and around the Calder valley finished up as dead-end branches, five of them were the remnants of much grander schemes for through lines. Probably the most ambitious of these was an LYR plan to shorten its 1841 route to Lancashire via Summit Tunnel by about five miles. This would be achieved by using the valley of the Ryburn, a tributary of the Calder, from Sowerby Bridge up to Rishworth, and then a four-mile tunnel under the Pennine watershed to Littleborough. Just how serious the LYR was about this is difficult to assess, as all that resulted was a 3¾-mile branch line. This was built to main line standards, however, and a new station was constructed at Sowerby Bridge, though without the extra platforms intended for the proposed through line.

Proposals for a branch had begun much earlier, and were included in the ill-fated WRUR scheme, but were left out of the Bill put to Parliament in 1846. It was another eighteen years before the idea was revived by the LYR, this time for a slightly shorter branch, just under three miles up the Ryburn valley to Ripponden. Despite opposition from local landowners, the Act for the line was passed in 1865, but it was eight years before work began. By this time, an Act for an extension to Rishworth had been passed as the first stage of the proposed cut-off to Littleborough. However, construction problems with landslips and the 593-yard Scar Head Tunnel delayed opening to Ripponden until 1878. At last, on August 5th, the first passenger trains ran, without an official ceremony although the village of Ripponden greeted the first arrival with cannons booming and church bells ringing and, later, with the village brass band, and a meal for dignitaries at the Golden Lion. On opening day more passengers were carried than on any other LYR branch, while work on the extension to Rishworth was well under way. This opened in 1881, with rather more subdued celebrations, and a survey was carried out the following year for the proposed line to Littleborough.

However, this appears to have been the last of that scheme, and the Rishworth line was operated as a branch, with an extra station added at Triangle in 1885. Services in 1900 were eleven trains each way on weekdays, with two extra on Saturdays and five on Sundays. In 1907 the LYR introduced on this line (and

Hughes railmotor no 8 waits at Sowerby Bridge with a Rishworth branch train. (Author's collection)

the Stainland branch) the first of its railmotor services in Yorkshire. The LYR railmotor consisted of a tiny 0–4–0 tank engine originally attached to a single coach, with at its far end a special compartment equipped with remote control gear. This allowed the train on its return journey to be driven from the coach, the fireman staying with the engine. The coach's seats were reversible, and there were steps that could be let down at halts without platforms. One of these was built on the branch at Watson Crossing, and an extra platform was added on the branch at Sowerby Bridge, so that the trains no longer needed to reverse out of the station.

The railmotors allowed an increase in services to eighteen weekday trains each way in 1921, but the start of a Rishworth–Halifax bus service five years later led to the end of the line's passenger service, which came on Saturday 6th July 1929. Goods services and occasional excursions onto the line continued into the 1950s. The last railtour was in 1951 and, the following year, BR closed the extension to Rishworth. Freight to

A railmotor waits at Ripponden station, which was built on a shelf on the valley side. (Lens of Sutton Association)

Ripponden lingered on until 1958, when the line was closed completely and it was dismantled by 1962. Much of the route can be traced and walked in places, but the surviving remains, the bricked-up portals of Scar Head Tunnel and the platform at Rishworth, are barely accessible.

Stainland

Unlike most of these branches, the LYR line to Stainland & Holywell Green was not meant to be part of an ambitious scheme. Instead it was built solely as a 1¾-mile branch south from the Calder Valley main line at Greetland, serving several villages and woollen mills. This makes all the more surprising its excessive engineering (a double-track line, two viaducts totalling 27 arches and two substantial stations) and total cost of £140,000. It opened for passengers to West Vale and Stainland

81

An LYR branch line scene at Stainland & Holywell Green station around 1907. Note the rear driving compartment on the railmotor coach. (Stations UK)

('& Holywell Green' was added later) on 1st January 1875, and for goods nine months later.

The Halifax tram system reached West Vale in 1905, which prompted the LYR to introduce a railmotor service on 1st March 1907. A halt was added at Rochdale Road, Greetland, more convenient for West Vale's centre, and services to and from Halifax increased to seventeen daily on weekdays by 1910. However, the trams reached Stainland in 1921, and the branch passenger service was unable to compete, finishing on 21st September 1929. Goods services survived for another 30 years.

The trackbed is remarkably intact for a line abandoned for almost 50 years. However, all the stations have disappeared, along with the mills at Stainland, where the route is used for vehicle access into the works that replaced them. The line can be walked across the 179-yard Stainland Viaduct, but West Vale Viaduct, longer at 230 yards and still intact, is sealed off. Access

West Vale was the branch's only intermediate station. (Author's collection)

is then possible for the rest of the line northwards, except for a break caused by a missing bridge at Rochdale Road.

Holmfirth

This small Pennine town was made famous by the television series *Last of the Summer Wine*, but its 1¾-mile railway branch had fewer claims to fame. It was built together with the Huddersfield–Penistone line, which it joined at Brockholes Junction, by the Huddersfield & Sheffield Junction Railway (H&SJR). Both lines opened on 1st July 1850, with the Huddersfield–Penistone line's inaugural journey an ambitious trip to Rowsley in Derbyshire for a visit to Chatsworth House. So many people attempted to board this excursion, that the first train from Holmfirth, at 11.25 am, became a 12-noon departure from Huddersfield to Penistone carrying the excess passengers.

Most of those from Holmfirth returned from Penistone in time for the opening day's celebratory tea!

The line qualifies as one of those for which extensions were intended, but it is not clear how serious these plans were. Certainly the line had been laid as double-track, and an Act had been obtained in 1847 for an extension to Holmbridge two miles further up the valley. This was not built, and nothing came of probably fanciful plans to reach the Woodhead line at Crowden, or even more unrealistically the Midland at Hathersage. Instead the line settled down as a country branch of the LYR, which had handled its workings from the start. Not that this was without incident, as the H&SJR appears to have left a legacy of problems with viaducts. On the Holmfirth branch, these came with the Mytholmbridge Viaduct, originally built as a timber trestle structure more suited to the American 'Wild West'. It had collapsed during construction, and a second trestle bridge

A view of Mytholmbridge Viaduct as shown on a postcard dated 1918. (Author's collection)

84

Although sited on the Huddersfield–Penistone line, Lockwood (seen here in 1966) was both a stop and a depot for the Holmfirth, Meltham and Clayton West branches. (Author's collection)

A similar view 40 years later shows Lockwood down to a single line and platform for the surviving Huddersfield–Sheffield trains. (Author)

The station house still survives as a residence at the Holmfirth terminus site.
(Author)

inspired little confidence. The LYR agreed to replace it with a stone viaduct, which was being built alongside the timber structure in 1865. On 3rd December, the stone viaduct's no 7 pier collapsed, bringing the rest down with it along with the trestle. The local corn miller averted a disaster by waking the Holmfirth stationmaster in time to prevent a train setting off from Huddersfield. The line was out of action for over fifteen months, not re-opening until March 1867.

The branch had two stations, at Thongsbridge and at the Holmfirth terminus, where (up to 1938) the turntable at the end of the platform made it a popular subject for model railway layouts! By 1879 there were nine weekday trains to and from Huddersfield (several running through to Bradford, Leeds or Halifax), with an extra Saturday train and three on Sundays. The branch appeared to withstand road competition better than most, but Sunday workings had ended by 1942 when there were still thirteen weekday trains. Only in the 1950s did the service decline markedly to only four trains a day, but these were still well patronised, and there was an outcry at BR's proposal in June 1959 to withdraw them. The last trains ran on Saturday 31st October 1959; ironically BR was already running the dieselised service the protestors had wanted for the Holmfirth line on its Huddersfield–Penistone route.

Special trips on and off the branch continued until 1965, but in that year goods services ended and track lifting began. Thongsbridge station was demolished and, in 1976, Mytholmbridge Viaduct was blown up, with considerable difficulty, and resulting in the temporary blocking of the stream. However, Holmfirth station largely survives, both the station house and goods warehouse being converted into residences.

Meltham

This 3½-mile line was a purely local affair, built by the LYR from its Huddersfield–Penistone line to provide access to the thread mills owned by the Brooke family at Meltham. Unfortunately, the survey for the line failed to discover water-bearing shale and sandstone beds, which resulted in numerous landslips along the route. Work started in 1864, three years after Parliamentary approval, but a proposed opening date in May 1867 had to be postponed, as over 60 wagonloads of spoil were still being removed daily from continuing landslips. When the line did open for freight in August 1868, further rock falls soon closed it again. Only after massive retaining walls were built (including one believed to be the most substantial on the LYR), did the line eventually open for passengers on 5th July 1869. A special train of eleven coaches from Huddersfield was the first onto the branch, and a dinner was provided for dignitaries at the Rose and Crown in Netherton.

The line ran from Meltham Junction on the Huddersfield–Penistone line past Beaumont Park, where a halt was planned but never built, to Woodfield. Here a station was opened in 1874

A view of Netherton station taken about 1895. (Author's collection)

but lasted only a month before closure. The line's two more long-lasting intermediate stations were at Netherton and Healey House. Netherton served a sizeable village, but the latter was provided for the nearby house of the same name, and Crosland Hall on the other side of the station. A halt was built at Meltham Mills, usually called 'Spink station', which closed with the end of thread making at the works in 1934. Finally, there was the terminus at Meltham, from which a service, referred to locally as the 'Meltham Coddy', of eleven trains a day (plus an extra on Saturdays) ran to Halifax, Mirfield or Bradford in 1895.

The line continued as a small country branch, away from the threat of electric trams from Huddersfield, until the mills' closure in 1934. The complex, however, was taken over for the manufacture of tractors by David Brown. This led to a massive increase in freight movements on the railway, especially during the Second World War, when the workforce grew to 2,500 for work on aero gears. In addition, whole trains of armoured vehicles were sent from all over the country to the works for gear box repairs. When tractor production resumed after the war, the line stayed busy for freight, but passengers had been lost to the buses, many rail journeys not managing a single passenger from the branch.

BR withdrew the passenger service on 23rd May 1949, and the line was converted to freight operations, principally David Brown 'tractor trains' which ran two or three times a day with 40 or more wagons. Special trains ran from 1949 to 1961 taking tractors to the Royal Show. Despite this traffic, BR closed the line in 1965, forcing the tractor output onto the roads until the works closed in 1988. Meltham station building stood for many years, including a spell as the works' despatch office, but has now been demolished though the station house survives in

Meltham station is seen here after closure to passengers in 1949. (D. Lawrence)

Station Street. Elsewhere little is left, but much of the trackbed can still be followed, for example on a shelf above Huddersfield's Beaumont Park.

Clayton West

The last LYR branch from the Huddersfield–Penistone line was something of an oddity, not least because it kept its passenger trains until 1983. Its terminus at the small town of Clayton West was also well to the south-east, and closer to Barnsley than Huddersfield. This helps explain its attraction for railway-builders, although all that resulted was over 60 years of unsuccessful schemes for a through line. These began with a proposal in 1846, for a link from the Huddersfield–Penistone line through Clayton West to the GNR south of Doncaster. No further schemes were suggested until the LNWR obtained an Act for its Kirkburton branch in 1863 (see next section). This attracted the Midland, which saw the possibility of a Barnsley–Clayton West–Kirkburton line to give access to Huddersfield, and alarmed by this potential competition, the LYR offered the Midland running powers via Penistone. The Midland dropped its scheme, and the LYR promised instead to provide Clayton West with a 3½-mile branch from the Huddersfield–Penistone line. This passed through Parliament in 1866, but the LYR was reluctant to make a start, even suggesting in the following year that the branch line proposal might be dropped.

Eventually there was a sod-cutting ceremony in 1872, followed by a lunch in Skelmanthorpe schoolroom. Afterwards, the well-known LYR official Thomas Normington raised the prospect of an extension to Darton, north of Barnsley, much to the annoyance of his employers. Finally the branch opened, at short notice, in 1879, with a wooden station building at Skelmanthorpe and a more substantial stone one at Clayton West. Initial services were six weekday trains to and from Huddersfield. In 1892 the LYR belatedly revived the Clayton West–Darton extension idea in conjunction with an

*Fowler class 4P 2–6–4T no 42405 at the Clayton West terminus in 1952.
(C.H.A. Townley, courtesy of J.A. Peden)*

*A wintry scene at Clayton West in December 1981 with a DMU for
Huddersfield. (Author's collection)*

independent scheme to link Barnsley with Sutton, near Retford. The LYR proposal for a 3¾-mile line with a 1,936-yard tunnel passed through Parliament, but was abandoned in 1899 after the withdrawal of the Barnsley–Retford project. Finally in 1906 the Clayton West & Darton Light Railway was backed by the LYR, but this scheme disappeared during the First World War.

The branch continued in use for passenger trains to Huddersfield, with some continuing on to Bradford. In 1925 there were nine weekday trains, but these had declined to six in the 1950s and four by closure in 1983. This was on Saturday 22nd January with the trains crowded, mostly with photographers. General goods traffic had already virtually ended and, with the local collieries switching to road transport, the line closed completely later that year, with the track lifted in 1986. However, within five years there was permission to put it

'Santa Special' time on the Kirklees Light Railway in December 2005 with Badger, *an 0–6–4 saddle tank loco specially built for this line in 1991. (Author)*

back, or at least a 15-inch gauge version. This was for the Kirklees Light Railway, opened to the public in 1991 with one mile of track at Clayton West, then an extension to Skelmanthorpe the following year.

Now the light railway extends over the whole length of the former branch, to a picnic/play area at Shelley. There is a halt at Cuckoo's Nest, plus 'stations' at Skelmanthorpe and Clayton West (not the originals, which had been demolished). Passenger trains run daily from late May to early September, Saturdays and Sundays only for the rest of the year, hauled by specially-built miniature locomotives. This 'revival' offers a small but interesting addition to the railway scene, if not quite what the branch's original promoters intended!

Kirkburton

This 4½-mile line was the LNWR's only branch in the Huddersfield area. It left the Huddersfield–Leeds main line at Deighton, and followed minor valleys to a terminus actually at Highburton, though named after Kirkburton half a mile away. Construction began in 1865, and the line opened on 6th October 1867, when 2–4–0T loco no 37 *Hawk*, 'decorated with evergreens', left Huddersfield station at 7 am. Construction had not been straightforward, with two deep cuttings requiring the removal of half a million cubic yards of material, and the construction of two viaducts, one of six arches over the Beldon Brook, and the seven-arch Whitacre Mill Viaduct over the River Colne and the Huddersfield Broad Canal (also known as Sir John Ramsden's Canal).

The LNWR had obtained enough land for two tracks and intended the line to become part of a through route towards Barnsley, while relying on other companies to achieve this. When the Midland withdrew from its proposed line through Clayton West in 1866, only the Hull & Barnsley (1882) and the Hull & North Western Junction Railway (1887) came up with schemes, both with no chance of being realised. The line was left operating as a branch from Huddersfield for its 63 years of passenger service, initially with six weekday trains to Kirkburton station. Three months after opening, further stations were opened at Fenay Bridge (which added '& Lepton' in 1897) and Kirkheaton, with a final addition at Deighton in 1871. Chemical works near the latter were an important source of traffic for the line, sending out over one million tons of acids and explosives during the First World War, along with over ten million hand grenades from a fireworks factory at Fenay Bridge.

In 1925 passenger services (known locally as 'Kirkburton Dick') were still at their peak with eleven weekday trains and two more on Saturdays. During the following year's General Strike, a volunteer crew took 0–6–2T no 189 to Kirkburton without enough water for the return journey; it is said the loco had to stay at the terminus until the strike was over! By this time the line was unable to compete with buses serving the village centres, especially Kirkburton and, in 1930, it was one of 23 branches closed by the LMS, the last scheduled passenger trains

Kirkheaton station in 1958, 28 years after closure to passengers. (Stations UK)

running on 26th July. The branch had always seen many holiday and excursion trips, the first a mill outing to Liverpool in 1868 for three shillings and sixpence, and these continued up to 1939. In the 1950s and early 60s the line was popular with enthusiasts' railtours, but in 1965 BR closed the line to goods traffic and lifted the track the following year, except for the first mile serving the chemical works at Deighton. This was abandoned in 1971, with a new Deighton station provided on the main line in 1982. The route is substantially intact, with both viaducts still in place, but currently only walkable in places although there are plans to convert it into a cycleway.

Dewsbury (Market Place)

A branch from the Calder Valley main line into central Dewsbury was one of the WRUR schemes abandoned by the LYR, relying instead on its 'Dewsbury' station 1¼ miles away (renamed Thornhill in 1851). However, by 1856 the LYR, worried by competition from the LNWR and from GNR-backed schemes, had revived the scheme for a branch. In 1861 an Act was obtained for a 1¼-mile line from Dewsbury East junction to a station site at Dewsbury's Market Place. Despite the short length, construction was still under way in 1865 when the LYR realised a quarter-mile fork west towards Thornhill was also needed. This was added without Parliamentary approval, the LYR also showing a cavalier attitude to the need for a time extension (a goods train was run in August 1866 to claim the line had been completed). It was April 1867 before the line opened to passenger traffic.

The completed branch extended north from east and west connections near Thornhill, and crossed a 135-ft girder bridge over the Calder into the station. It was flanked by four huge goods warehouses, two of them for 'shoddy', the coarse woollen cloth made from waste, which was a speciality of Dewsbury (and neighbouring Batley). Initially passenger services were nineteen weekday trains to Mirfield, Wakefield or Thornhill, with eight on Sundays, but by 1869 there were ten to

Dewsbury Market Place station in 1928, two years before closure to passengers. (Stations UK)

An earlier view of Thornhill station, the destination for many trains from Dewsbury Market Place. (Author's collection)

twelve additional trains to Bradford using the newly opened Thornhill–Heckmondwike line.

Sunday services ended in 1917 but the line kept busy, especially during Dewsbury holidays in late July, up to 1930. The LMS claimed closure to passengers would save £1,484 a year, and the last trains ran on Saturday 29th November. The final scheduled train was the 10.40 pm shuttle back from Thornhill, although a Rugby League excursion returning from Hull was the last passenger train at the station. The building was used by businesses for a time, before it was bought by Dewsbury Corporation and demolished in 1938–9. The goods facilities remained intact into the 1950s, but finally closed in 1961. The first half-mile from Dewsbury East junction remains in use for industrial purposes, but all traces in central Dewsbury have been lost.

Birstall

The easternmost of the LNWR branches was all that resulted from ambitious schemes to reach Bradford from the south-east in the 1850s and 60s. The 1¾-mile line had been authorised along with the Leeds–Dewsbury main line in 1845, but the LNWR appeared reluctant to make a start, and the line did not open until 1852. However, it had reached within six miles of central Bradford, and the LNWR backed the nominally independent Dewsbury, Batley, Gomersal & Bradford Railway scheme to complete the link. This failed in Parliament in 1861, and although the LB&HJR (see Chapter 4) did get an Act involving use of the branch the same year, it was repealed in 1862. Instead the LB&HJR built its own line just to the east, the LNWR didn't reach Bradford, and the branch to Birstal (the historic spelling) remained a backwater.

The line ran from Batley to a terminus in Birstal and opened on 30th September 1852, with initial services, known locally as the 'Birstal Coddy', of five weekday trains to and from Dewsbury. In 1872 an intermediate station opened at Carlinghow and, by 1899, there were fifteen weekday trains, with two extra on Saturdays, but by then most trains ran only to

The last enthusiasts' trip on the branch was hauled by a similar ex-LYR 0–6–0 loco to no 52575, seen here at Sowerby Bridge. (Author's collection)

Little is left of the line except this fine bridge which now carries the Batley Cycleway over a track by Wilton Park. (Author)

Batley. That was, however, the peak for this line; next year Upper Birstal opened on the Leeds New Line and, in 1905, trams on the nearby main road were electrified. By 1910 train services were down to four a day, and finished completely as a 'temporary' wartime measure at the end of 1916.

The branch continued in use for freight for another 46 years. Even by 1950 there were still morning and afternoon goods trains, which continued until 16th June 1952, when the last 'passenger' train ran – a brake van special organised by Wakefield Railfans Club and hauled by ex-LYR loco no 52515. The former Birstall station was for years used by an adjacent mill, but eventually demolished; now housing occupies both station sites. However, just half a mile of the former route is still accessible to the public as the Batley Cycleway.

7
Pennines and Coalfield – the Great Central Railway

The Woodhead line/Penistone–Sheffield Victoria/
Mexborough–Barnsley/Barnsley–Sheffield/
The GCR through Rotherham/Stairfoot–Nostell/
The South Yorkshire Joint Railway

Express working on the GCR – one of Robinson's handsome class 11B 4–4–0 locos, seen here as LNER no 5108, heads south between Penistone and Sheffield in 1923. (A.G. Ellis)

The Woodhead line

The Great Central Railway (GCR) was the name adopted by the Manchester, Sheffield & Lincolnshire Railway (MS&LR) in 1897. The company already had a substantial network in the

Yorkshire coalfield area, largely through its acquisition of the South Yorkshire Railway (see later), but its start in the area was with the Sheffield, Ashton-under-Lyne & Manchester Railway (SA&MR), one of the companies that formed the MS&LR in 1847.

The SA&MR promoted the first successful scheme for a railway connection between Sheffield and Manchester, obtaining its Act in 1837. This was for a 42-mile line using the Don valley to the east, and Longdendale and the Etherow valley in the west, but still requiring the building of the three-mile long Woodhead Tunnel at close to 1,000 ft above sea level to cross the Pennine watershed. Only the section east of the tunnel lies in Yorkshire; the stretch to Penistone is covered here, with Penistone–Sheffield to follow. The construction of the line began from both ends, the eastern section from Sheffield to the tunnel being completed in July 1845. Five months later the single-track tunnel was ready, and the first train ran over the whole route from Sheffield to Manchester on 22nd December 1845. Building the tunnel had cost the lives of 26 of the 1,500 navvies that had worked on it in appalling conditions. Within the section being considered here, stations were initially provided at Dunford

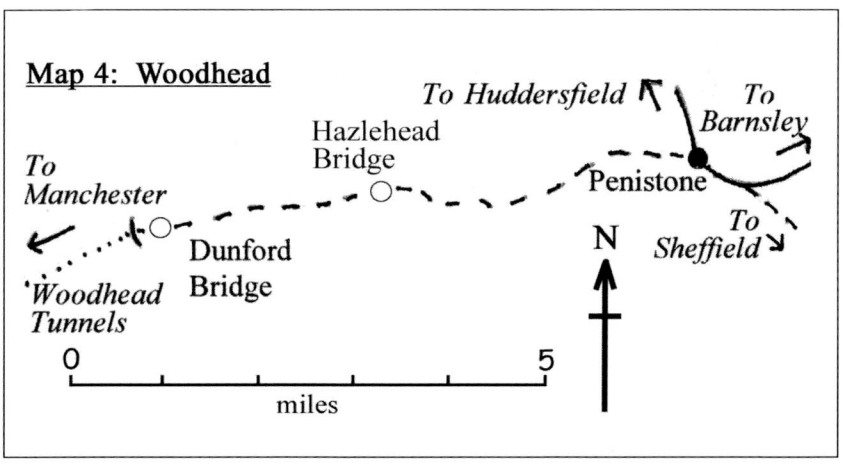

Map 4: Woodhead

Bridge and Penistone, plus in 1846 Hazlehead (Hazlehead Bridge from 1850).

After the formation of the MS&LR in 1847, one of the new company's first acts was to sanction a second single-bore tunnel, completed in 1852. Despite improved welfare conditions, the death toll was 28, largely due to a cholera outbreak. By 1900 the line was overloaded with passenger trains queueing to get amongst the never-ending freight trains carrying Yorkshire coal westwards and returning empty. Passenger trains from Liverpool and Manchester to Sheffield had been augmented by expresses heading for the London extension opened in 1899 by the GCR.

Electrification was first mentioned in 1913, when the GCR's Locomotive Superintendent, John Robinson, visited the USA and noted the 1,500-volt dc system in use there. His idea was to use a similar system on the infamous Worsborough Bank section of the freight line from the Barnsley area to Penistone, which supplied most of Woodhead's coal trains. The plan was abandoned due to the cost, but the idea of this particular electric system was carried through to the LNER scheme of the 1930s. This was for electrification from Sheffield, Wath and Barnsley to Penistone, and through Woodhead to Manchester, at an estimated cost of £2½ million including 88 locos, only one of which had been built before work was halted by the Second World War. Work resumed in 1946, but now the deteriorating condition of the Woodhead tunnels forced the LNER to plan for replacing them at a cost of a further £2.8 million. The escalating cost of the whole scheme (£12¼ million by 1950) led BR to cut back the project drastically, especially the number of locos. Even so the new double-track tunnel alone cost £4.6 million.

By January 1955, electric services between Sheffield and Manchester were fully operational, but in 1960 the through passenger services from Manchester and Sheffield to London Marylebone ended. Although Beeching did not recommend closure for the Woodhead line, in 1967 BR proposed giving freight the priority on the line, by switching passenger trains to the Hope Valley route. After a two-year inquiry, consent for the

By 1960 the electrics had taken over – here class EM1 no 26041 has just passed Hazlehead Bridge station with a westbound goods train. (D.L. Chatfield)

withdrawal of passenger services was given in 1969. On 4th January 1970 the last timetabled passenger train ran, and Dunford Bridge and the ex-GCR platforms at Penistone closed (Hazlebridge Bridge had shut in 1950).

Despite the claims for freight, many railwaymen thought the real reason for the withdrawal of passenger services was the incompatibility of Woodhead's 1,500 volt dc system with the 25kV ac alternative being developed elsewhere on BR. This of course applied equally to freight, and when the decline in coal shipments, plus a policy of using other routes, had considerably reduced goods trains, BR exercised its right to close the line. The last freight train was the Harwich–Liverpool Speedlink service on 18th July 1981, after which the line shut completely. Even the single line left through the tunnel was removed in 1986, and the portals were sealed off. Now the whole length of trackbed from

Ex-LNER class A3 Pacific no 60104 Solario *heads a London Marylebone–Manchester London Road express into Dunford Bridge in 1954 – note the signs of electrification. (Author's collection)*

An eastbound freight double-headed by no 76013 and no 76014 heads though the GCR side of Penistone station in the 1970s. (Travel Lens Photographic)

Today the GCR's platforms, island building and canopy have all gone, leaving only the main building (now business units) and the Sheffield–Huddersfield line out-of-sight to the right. (Author)

Both the station building and stationmaster's house at Hazlehead Bridge survive as residences overlooking the Trans Pennine Trail – the new use for the former trackbed. (Author)

the site of Dunford Bridge station, through the remaining buildings at Hazlehead Bridge, to Penistone is used by walkers and cyclists as part of the Trans Pennine Trail.

Penistone–Sheffield Victoria

This section was opened in 1845 as part of the SA&MR line from Manchester via Woodhead, following the course of the River Don south towards Sheffield. Only from Deepcar was the valley wide enough for the railway to follow it, and the first five miles included the four-arch Rumtickle Viaduct and the 350-yard Thurgoland Tunnel. By the time the line further west was operational through Woodhead Tunnel, stations had been opened at Oxspring, Thurgoland, Wortley, Deepcar, Oughty Bridge and Wadsley Bridge, with a later addition at Neepsend

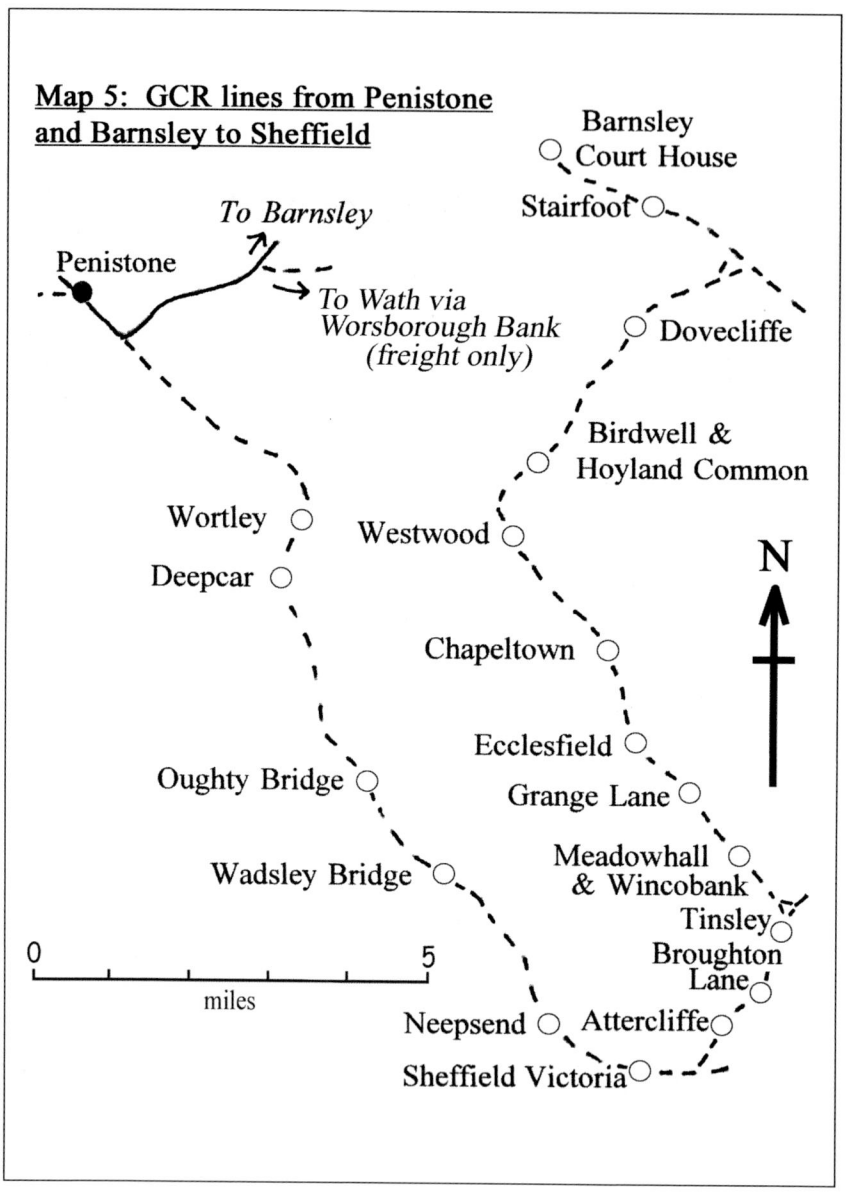

Map 5: GCR lines from Penistone and Barnsley to Sheffield

Barnsley
Court House

Stairfoot

To Barnsley

Penistone

→ *To Wath via Worsborough Bank (freight only)*

Dovecliffe

Birdwell & Hoyland Common

Wortley

Westwood

Deepcar

N

Chapeltown

Ecclesfield

Oughty Bridge

Grange Lane

Meadowhall & Wincobank

Wadsley Bridge

Tinsley

Broughton Lane

0   5

miles

Neepsend   Attercliffe

Sheffield Victoria

Wortley station in the early years of the 20th century. (Author's collection)

A century later, the former Wortley station buildings now overlook the Upper Don Trail. (Author)

(1888–1940). The first Sheffield terminus was a single platform with a wooden shed at Bridgehouses, but in 1851 the MS&LR opened a new station, Sheffield Victoria, on a through line out towards Gainsborough and Lincoln. This comprised a single island platform with bays at both ends, with a 400-ft glass and iron roof covering the buildings. A new roof was provided in 1865, and an additional platform in 1874, with further extensions in 1906–8 and 1937.

Destinations south and east of Sheffield Victoria were greatly extended by the construction of lines out to Rotherham (1864–8), Annesley (for access to Nottingham) in 1890–2, and the London extension south from Annesley opened in 1899. At the northern end of this section, the line at Penistone had been joined by the Huddersfield & Sheffield Junction Railway in 1850, bringing in trains from Halifax and Bradford. By 1905 the Penistone–Sheffield section was dealing with GCR express

Sheffield Victoria in 1956, with ex-LNER class B1 4–6–0 no 61231 and in the distance electric loco EM2 no 27006. (D.L. Chatfield)

One of the few tunnels in the area available for public access is at Thurgoland; this was an extra bore put in for the Woodhead electrification. (Author)

traffic from Liverpool and Manchester to London Marylebone (and GNR expresses to King's Cross), plus trains to Grimsby, Cleethorpes and the Norfolk coast, as well as excursion workings to Plymouth and 'boat trains' to Hull and Harwich. There were also local stopping services from Manchester and Penistone, five and six respectively on weekdays in 1922. However, these were the first to go; Thurgoland and Oxspring stations had been short-lived, Wortley shut in 1955, and local stopping services ended in 1959 with the closure of Deepcar, Oughty Bridge and Wadsley Bridge (except for football excursions to the nearby Sheffield Wednesday ground at Hillsborough). The London–Manchester service stopped the next year, and passenger trains through Woodhead in 1970. The Sheffield–Penistone–Huddersfield service continued to use this section until 1983, when it was switched to run via Barnsley.

Up to 1983, these trains had passed through the site of Sheffield Victoria station, where the rundown of services had begun in 1960, when the ex-GCR line north of Nottingham lost its through workings. By 1965 most local services had switched to Sheffield Midland, and in 1970 Victoria closed with the end of passenger services via Woodhead. Now nothing remains at the site, except the ex-railway hotel and the restored memorial to the 1,304 men of the GCR who died in the First World War. Eight miles of the line to Penistone remain in use as a single-track branch, serving the steelworks at Stocksbridge and passing the remains of Oughty Bridge and Deepcar stations. After a short gap before the former Wortley station, the rest of the trackbed is now a route for walkers, cyclists and horse riders as part of the Upper Don Trail.

Mexborough–Barnsley

In 1845, at the height of the 'Railway Mania', no fewer than 23 schemes were proposed for the Doncaster area. Only ten of these reached Parliament, including one from a forerunner of the South Yorkshire Railway (SYR). It was rejected, but among the successful proposals was that of the Sheffield, Rotherham, Barnsley, Wakefield, Huddersfield & Goole Railway (SRBWH&GR) for a link between Mexborough, in the Don Valley, and Barnsley. In 1847 the SYR reached an agreement with the SRBWH&GR to purchase the latter's routes south of Barnsley, and obtained an Act for the Mexborough–Barnsley line. The next year the SYR sought a link from Barnsley west to Penistone, but this was given to the MS&LR, which eventually completed the line in 1859.

The SYR line from Mexborough to the SRBWH&GR's Barnsley station (later called Exchange by the LYR) opened in 1851 (see map 8). Rudimentary stations were provided at Wath, Wombwell and Ardsley for a Doncaster–Barnsley passenger service originally operated by the GNR, as the SYR was more concerned with the movement of coal from local collieries. The two companies came close to amalgamation but, in 1853, the GNR cut its passenger service to one a day, leaving the SYR

Ex-LNER class C14 4–4–2 no 67445 (built by the GCR in 1907) at Doncaster – this loco worked the Penistone–Barnsley–Doncaster trains on the last day of passenger services in 1959. (D.L. Chatfield)

struggling to cope with locos and coaches borrowed from the Midland. The SYR ended up leased, not by the GNR, but by the MS&LR (which had already absorbed the SRBWH&GR) in 1864, and taken over completely ten years later.

The MS&LR undertook improvements, including the move to Barnsley's Court House station (see next section), also rebuilding the stations at Wath and Wombwell, and resiting Ardsley station (with a name change to Stairfoot). The major development for freight came under the GCR, with the development of the huge marshalling yard by the line at Wath, opened in 1907 to deal primarily with coal shipments. Passenger services on the line were basically Penistone–Barnsley–Doncaster trains first introduced by the MS&LR in 1859; for example, in 1922, these comprised ten weekday trains with two on Sundays. The service changed little through to its

Wombwell's GCR station building replaced an earlier South Yorkshire Railway one in 1877 and closed along with Wath in 1959 (Stairfoot had shut two years earlier). (Author's collection)

withdrawal just short of its centenary in 1959. This caused much local bitterness as the trains had been popular and well-used, and removed most passenger trains from the route, although the last of these continued until 1970.

Passenger services returned to the Penistone–Barnsley section in 1983, but not the Mexborough–Barnsley stretch. Its freight services were greatly reduced by the closure of the Woodhead line in 1981, although Wath yard did not shut until 1986, after which the line went out of use completely. The route at Wath has disappeared, but four miles through Wombwell and Stairfoot have been reclaimed as part of the Trans Pennine Trail for walkers, cyclists and horse riders.

Barnsley–Sheffield

The SRBWH&GR began construction of its Barnsley–Sheffield line with a 2,278-yard tunnel at Birdwell in 1847, but work stopped the following year after 6,000 cubic yards had been excavated from six shafts. When the SYR resumed work on the line in 1851, local colliery owners wanted a surface route further east, and so the tunnel was abandoned. The new route climbed at 1 in 63 to Birdwell, and then descended at a similar gradient, leading to descriptions of it as a 'helter-skelter'. It ran from an east-facing junction at Aldam, on the Barnsley–Mexborough line, through stations at Smithley (later Dovecliffe) and High Royd, which only lasted a year, to Birdwell. Further stations were built at Westwood, Chapeltown, Ecclesfield, Grange Lane and Meadowhall & Wincobank, before the line joined the Midland into the original Sheffield terminus at the Wicker.

In 1860 the SYR began construction of a Sheffield extension, but its line into Victoria did not open until after the MS&LR takeover in 1864. There was an intermediate station at Broughton Lane, with Tinsley added in 1869 and Attercliffe two years later. The MS&LR doubled the original single line, replaced the stations at Westwood and Ecclesfield in 1876, and the following year opened a new connection at Aldam giving direct access to Barnsley's Court House station. This had been

Transport artist G.S. Cooper's painting of Court House station in 1948 with LNER B17 no 1669 Barnsley, *one of the 'Locomotives named after Football Clubs' series by Dawn Cover Productions. (Courtesy of Dave Cooper at www.cooperline.com)*

adapted from its previous use by the Midland in 1871–2, and was regarded as a great improvement on the LYR's station, famously described as a 'beastly hole'.

In 1897 the Midland extended its freight-only Chapeltown branch, which ran parallel to the ex-SYR line, through to Barnsley, and began a competing passenger service. The two routes survived into the BR era, but it was the older ex-SYR route that was closed as a duplication in 1953. Westwood station had already shut in 1940, and a sparse timetable and few passengers meant there was little protest. Excursions from the line continued for another six years, and its Sheffield extension remained in passenger use until 1966 for Sheffield–Rotherham trains. Goods traffic on the Chapeltown section was cut back progressively as collieries closed, finally ending in 1986. The

Broughton Lane, seen here in poor condition in 1987, was the last of the SYR's Sheffield extension stations to close in 1956, following Attercliffe (1927) and Tinsley (1951). (Author's collection)

route has since become a cycleway between Meadowhall and Ecclesfield, and sections are still walkable at Chapeltown and past Hoyland and Wombwell, but little else is left.

The ex-Midland Barnsley–Sheffield passenger service survives, but the fate of Court House station provides a postscript. Despite being regarded as the town's 'top station', BR claimed that repairs to the viaduct leading to it from the south would cost £200,000, and moved the remaining services to the ex-LYR Exchange station in 1960. After use as a parcels depot, Court House was demolished in 1970 and is now a car park, although the original courthouse building survives.

The courthouse building had found yet another use by 2005 – as a pub! (Author)

The GCR through Rotherham

This was yet another SYR project, although construction did not begin until after the MS&LR takeover in 1864. As the SYR had earlier absorbed the Don Navigation, alongside which the railway would largely run, no Act of Parliament was ever obtained. This led to problems where the line was to run under the 1838 Sheffield & Rotherham line, as the only possible route meant using the canal. The MS&LR was forced to divert the canal for half a mile, then fill in the bed and lay rails on its former course. This was one reason why the cost of the project more than trebled by 1867, when work was suspended. It resumed the following year, when the line reached a temporary terminus in Rotherham, but it was 1871 before it was completed to the SYR's original line at Mexborough. Even this was only achieved by using the 1863 Mexborough–Kilnhurst potteries branch.

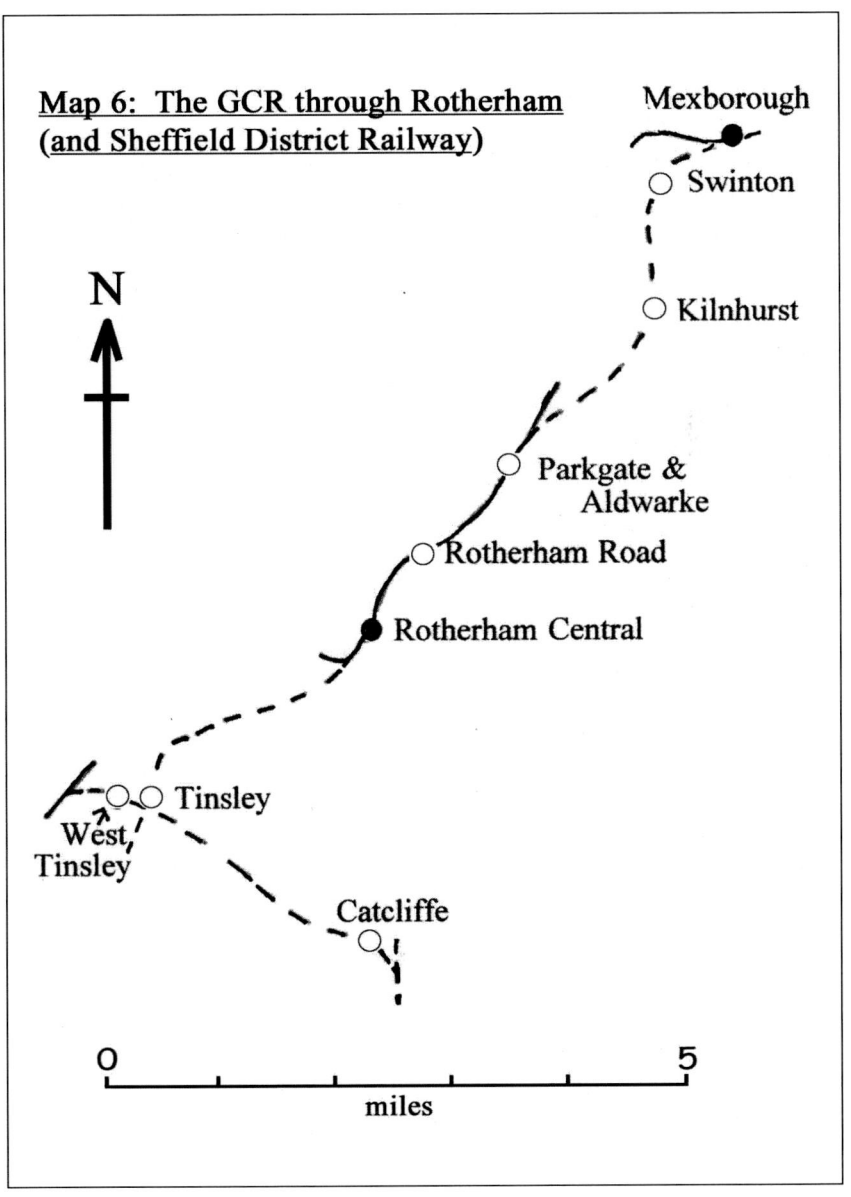

Map 6: The GCR through Rotherham (and Sheffield District Railway)

Rotherham Road, seen here in 1970, was an early closure to passengers in 1953, along with Parkgate & Aldwarke (1951) and Swinton (1958). (M.A. King)

The 7½-mile double-track line to Mexborough from the SYR Sheffield extension at Tinsley was never more than half a mile from the Midland route, which had been completed in 1840. Even its stations at Rotherham Central, which replaced the temporary station in 1874 and was known as Rotherham & Masborough from 1889 to 1950, Aldwarke (Parkgate & Aldwarke from 1895), Kilnhurst and Swinton duplicated those on the parallel line. Only the little-used Rotherham Road station was a genuine addition to the system. The Midland line always seems to have had more passenger traffic, especially on the Sheffield–Rotherham section; in 1922, for example, there were 45 weekday trains compared with 18 on the GCR line. The latter was at its busiest at holiday times, especially the 'Sheffield Works' July/August fortnight in the late 1940s and 50s, with departures from Victoria to the Yorkshire coast. However, in the 1960s, it was decided to concentrate all Sheffield services at the Midland station, and the ex-GCR services through Rotherham were withdrawn from 5th September 1966.

Rotherham Central station in 1947, nineteen years before closure. (Stations UK)

The replacement Rotherham Central station today. (Author)

The former GCR line was retained for freight for the many factories along the Don Valley, and in the 1980s there was a return to passenger use, at least at Rotherham. The ex-Midland station at Masborough was over a mile from the town centre, while the ex-GCR station, by then demolished, had been more centrally placed. BR decided to build a new 'Central' station on the old one's site, together with a new connection from the ex-Midland line. So from 11th May 1987 local trains have once again used the GCR's station site, together with 2½ miles of its line north to Rawmarsh. Through trains, meanwhile, speed through the remains of the Midland station, abandoned in 1988.

Stairfoot–Nostell

This line started as the Barnsley Coal Railway, promoted by local mine owners to serve pits north-east of the town, though with the intention of eventually reaching Wakefield. It was authorised in 1861 and was taken over by the SYR two years later. However, opposition from local landowners meant it was halted in 1870 at Applehaigh, five miles from Ardsley (later, Stairfoot) on the SYR Mexborough–Barnsley line, and so it was disparagingly referred to as the 'Barnsley Stump'. The MS&LR had acquired the line with its lease of the SYR in 1864, and obtained an Act in 1874 to extend it by a further five miles to Nostell on the Wakefield–Doncaster line. Links were also built to both Barnsley and the Midland main line. The latter connection was short-lived, but the extension to Nostell and the link to Barnsley allowed the MS&LR (and later GCR) to run a passenger service to Wakefield and Leeds starting in 1882 (see map 8).

Stations were built at Staincross on the original line to Applehaigh, plus Notton & Royston and Ryhill (Wintersett &

An early 20th century view of the station and staff at Ryhill. (Lens of Sutton Association)

Although Notton & Royston station closed in 1930, it was still in use for summer specials over 30 years later. (Stations UK)

Ryhill from 1927) on the extension to Nostell. By 1922 the GCR was running a basic service of five weekday Barnsley–Leeds trains, with one or two extra on Saturdays, but it was unable to compete with the much more direct Midland service from Cudworth. The LNER withdrew passenger services from the line on 22nd September 1930.

It remained in use for freight and a surprising amount of summer passenger traffic, when it was used for excursions and specials to relieve pressure on the Midland main line. This continued up to 1961, when the line closed north of Staincross (the connection into Barnsley had gone two years earlier). Colliery closures meant the rest of the line shut in 1967. Nothing has been left of the three stations, but the trackbed at the southern end is now largely used for footpaths in the Dearne Valley Park, and as part of the Royston and Carlton Boundary Walk.

The South Yorkshire Joint Railway

Although five companies owned this line (not to be confused with the South Yorkshire Railway dealt with previously), it was the GCR that operated most of its early passenger services. In 1902 all five were planning lines into the coalfield area south of

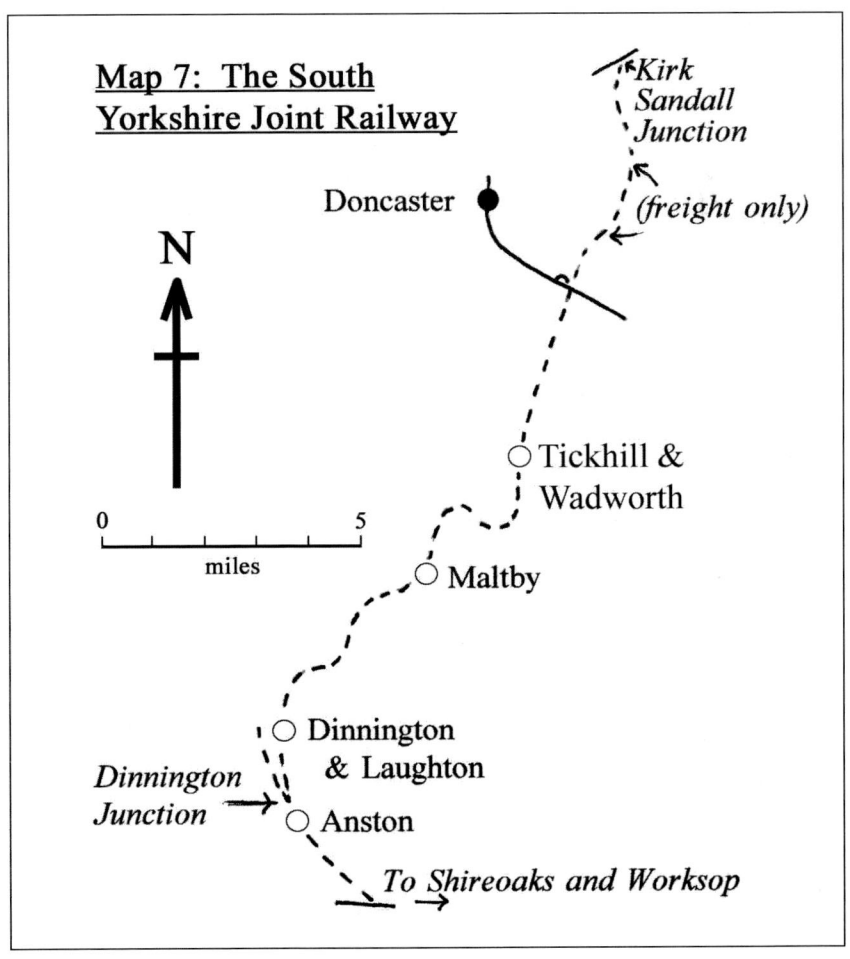

Map 7: The South Yorkshire Joint Railway

Doncaster. The GCR and Midland had already jointly taken over the Shireoaks, Laughton and Maltby project to gain an approach from the south, and aimed to continue north through Maltby, while the NER and LYR planned a similar joint line, and the GNR a line west from Bawtry. Sanity prevailed and all five companies agreed to combine in the South Yorkshire Joint Committee, established in 1904. Between 1905 and 1909, a 17½ mile line was built from the GCR/Midland joint line at Dinnington Junction to Kirk Sandall, north-east of Doncaster.

From its opening in 1909, the line concentrated on freight, chiefly the movement of coal, which reached over a million tons in 1913. Stations had been built at Tickhill & Wadworth, Maltby and Dinnington & Laughton, originally for goods, but passenger services were soon considered. These began in June and July 1910, with excursions to Doncaster and Cleethorpes and on 1st December regular passenger services began, with two GCR and two GNR trains each way between Doncaster and

GCR class 9K 4–4–2T no 1062 heads the first passenger train at Tickhill station in 1908 (although this was a trial run as passenger services did not begin until 1910). (Stations UK)

Shireoaks. Within a year the service was cut to three trains, all operated by the GCR, although in 1912 an extra station opened to passengers at Anston, on the GCR/Midland joint line. Even in 1913, the peak year for passenger numbers with over 60,000 booked at the line's stations, the service still lost money.

In June 1917 the Committee reduced the passenger service to Saturdays only as a wartime economy measure, and was reluctant to reinstate a full service when the war ended. Eventually, on 1st April 1920, weekday passenger trains ran once more, but only two trains a day, with a 'market special' and an evening train (from October) on Saturdays. A coal strike closed the line completely in 1921, after which passenger closure was discussed. The stumbling block was the major local landowner, Lord Scarborough, who had established a legal right to a permanent passenger service to Maltby. Reluctantly, the Committee continued the service, but axed the Saturday evening train in 1922. The General Strike of 1926 led to complete

The former station house at Tickhill is still in use as a residence. (Author)

Brookhouse Viaduct under repair in May 2006. Note the piers built for doubling of the track which never happened. (Author)

closure for fifteen months, and when the line reopened, a Sentinel steam railcar was tried without success. At last, after the service had been reduced to a single Worksop–Maltby–Worksop train a day, Lord Scarborough agreed to its withdrawal on 2nd December 1929. A final attempt in 1935 to restore passenger trains failed, but outward excursions continued until 1966, after which there were only a few railtours. The line has stayed in use for coal trains, though these are currently serving only the last remaining colliery at Maltby.

8
Hopes Unfulfilled – the Midland

The main line north to Normanton/ Links and branches

The Midland adapted Barnsley's courthouse for its station, shown here with class 1P 0–4–4T no 58075 on the shuttle service to Cudworth in 1950. (Author's collection)

The main line north to Normanton

It is very rare for an early main line to become a 'lost railway' but that has been the fate of 18½ miles of the oldest line featured in this book, George Hudson's North Midland Railway (NMR) from Derby to Leeds, which opened in 1840. Engineered by

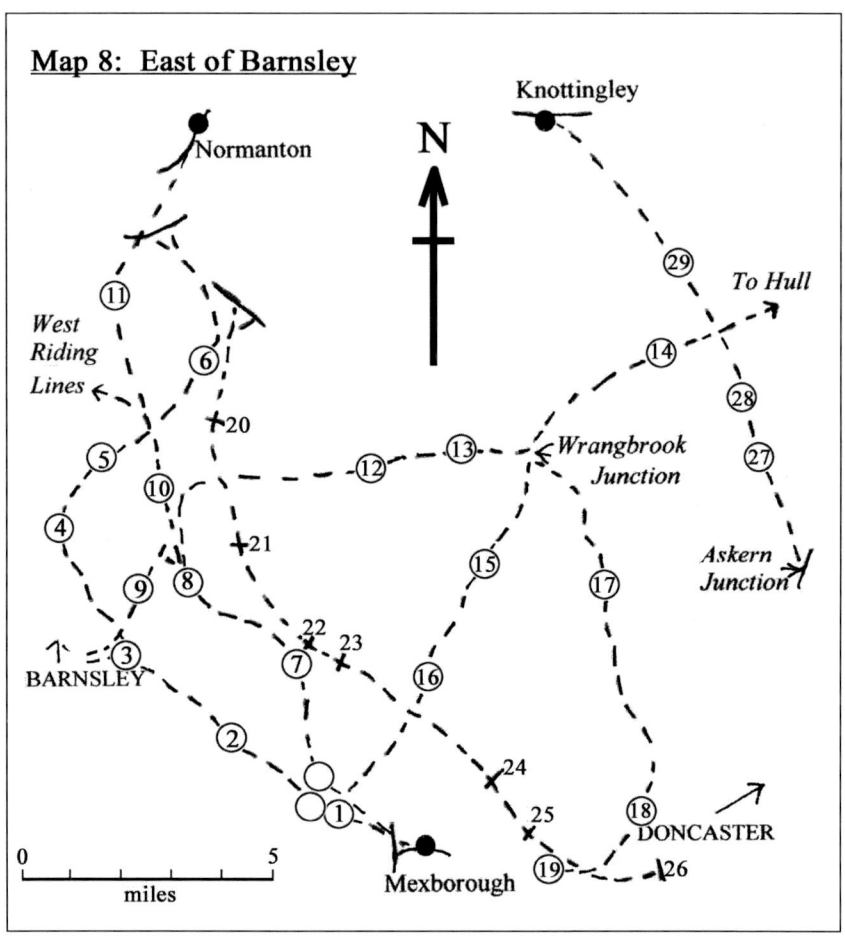

Map 8: East of Barnsley

George Stephenson, the line avoided high ground in following the Dearne valley northwards from Rotherham, though the 702-yard Chevet Tunnel was required to give access to the Calder valley at Normanton. However, this low-lying route missed most centres of population, including Barnsley and Wakefield. While stations were provided for villages at Wath, Darfield, and Royston (1841), the Barnsley station was at

130

KEY TO DISUSED STATIONS, MAP 8

GCR:
1 Wath (also stations for Midland and Hull & Barnsley)
2 Wombwell
3 Stairfoot (previously Ardsley)
4 Staincross
5 Notton & Royston
6 Ryhill

Midland:
7 Darfield
8 Cudworth
9 Monk Bretton
10 Royston & Notton
11 Sandal & Walton

Hull & Barnsley:
12 Hemsworth & S. Kirkby
13 Upton & N. Elmsall
14 Kirk Smeaton

15 Moorhouse & South Elmsall
16 Hickleton & Thurnscoe
17 Pickburn & Brodsworth
18 Sprotborough
19 Denaby & Conisbrough

DVR (all halts)
20 Ryhill
21 Grimethorpe
22 Great Houghton
23 Goldthorpe & Thurnscoe
24 Harlington
25 Denaby
26 Edlington

LYR:
27 Askern
28 Norton
29 Womersley

Cudworth 2½ miles away and 'Wakefield' at Oakenshaw 2 miles distant. Neither survived long under these names; the Barnsley station eventually became Cudworth, while Wakefield was renamed Oakenshaw in 1841. It closed in 1870, and was replaced by a station at Sandal & Walton (Walton from 1951) a mile to the south.

The line opened on Tuesday 30th June 1840, when a special train left Leeds for Derby carrying about 500 dignitaries in 35 carriages hauled by two of Stephenson's locomotives (plus two more at the rear). With a further 28 carriages added later, it took over five hours for the journey at an average speed of 14 mph. Better times, though still up to four hours, were achieved by the public services that began the next day with six trains each way on weekdays and four on Sundays. Services were similar in 1861 though by then there were connections and even some through trains to Scotland. These services received a major boost in 1876, when the Midland Railway (the successor to the NMR) completed its Settle–Carlisle line. This led to

131

The 'Thames-Clyde Express' was one of the line's 'named' passenger workings, here headed by ex-LMS Black Five 4–6–0 no 45404 south of Sheffield around 1960. (P. Wilson)

quadrupling of the tracks between Rotherham and Normanton from 1890, which necessitated the rebuilding of Darfield station on a new site 1,000 yards further north. At Cudworth the 1840 NMR 'Barnsley' station was demolished and a new station built with five platforms (plus one for the Hull & Barnsley line – see Chapter 9). Royston & Notton station was also replaced by a new one a mile to the south. Track improvements continued into the 1920s, when the LMS opened out Chevet Tunnel to create possibly Britain's deepest cutting at 110 ft and allow the final stretch of quadrupling.

The line was at its busiest up to 1914, but even twenty years later there was a service of twenty weekday trains each way on the Sheffield–Leeds line, along with long-distance trains, including the St Pancras to Scotland 'Thames-Clyde' and 'Thames-Forth' (later 'Waverley') expresses, the 'Yorkshireman' from Bradford to Marylebone and the Bradford–Paignton

A fine line-up of Stanier class 8F locos outside the last engine shed built by the LMS, opened at Royston in 1932. (N. Metcalfe/Northern Historical Images)

One of Royston shed's allocated class 8F locos in 1956, no 48473, heads a coal train through the station. (Author's collection)

A view of the second Royston & Notton station, probably taken around ten years after it opened in 1900. (Author's collection)

'Devonian'. All these except the 'Yorkshireman' were still running in 1960, but the Sheffield–Leeds service was down to ten on weekdays, with an equal number of un-named long-distance trains. However, the line was suffering from subsidence caused by coal mining and, in 1967, the long-distance trains were diverted away. The following year the Sheffield–Leeds service ended and the remaining stations closed (Walton had shut in 1961 and Darfield in 1963), along with Normanton engine shed.

Retired railwayman Frank Jolliffe remembered the precise day, 24th June 1929, that he began working for the LMS at Normanton as the telephone boy in the engine shed foreman's office. After a break he returned there and worked his way up as cleaner, fireman and passed fireman, able to do occasional turns as a driver. Normanton shed was primarily concerned with freight, hence the term for the town 'The Crewe of the Coalfields'. Frank remembered many freight trips along the ex-Midland line south to Swinton and Rotherham, and especially to Toton near Nottingham. Passenger workings from

Ex-LMS 2–6–4T no 42189 at Frank Jolliffe's first workplace, Normanton shed. (N. Metcalfe/Northern Historical Images)

Normanton shed were less common but did include the 6.21 am to Leeds, which then became the 8.35 stopping train back along the line to Sheffield. One memorable trip for Frank was when he fired a double-headed 'Thames-Clyde Express' from Leeds to Carlisle, a journey of 113 miles. He later left Normanton to become a driver at Wakefield shed, where he remembered trips on the former GNR line to Dewsbury, Batley and Bradford (as described in Chapter 4) before finishing his career at Healey Mills diesel depot.

Subsidence problems on the line the trains had been diverted to in 1967 – the former Swinton & Knottingley Railway – led to north-east–south-west trains being rerouted through Cudworth in 1972. Ten years later, they were switched back, possibly due to the ex-Midland line's lack of a local stopping service, and in 1986 it was severed as a through route. The line south through Cudworth was kept for coal traffic from Grimethorpe Colliery

A single line serving a glassworks near Barnsley is all that is left of the six tracks at the site of the earlier Royston station. (Author)

until that closed in 1996, then cut back to Cudworth North Junction for freight to glassworks at Monk Bretton near Barnsley. This still continued in 2005 with thrice-weekly deliveries of sand. Now a single freight line occupies the trackbed for eight miles south of Wakefield, but beyond Cudworth only earthworks mark the route of this former main line.

Links and branches

Three lines branching off the former Midland main line have also closed to passenger traffic. The southernmost of these is the 3½-mile link between Treeton on the main line and Brightside on the Sheffield & Rotherham Railway of 1838. It was built as the Sheffield District Railway by the Lancashire, Derbyshire & East Coast Railway (LD&ECR). This company's plan was for an

Tinsley Road (renamed West Tinsley in 1907) was one of two passenger stations on the Sheffield District Railway. (Author's collection)

ambitious £5 million scheme to link Warrington to the North Sea at Sutton-on-Sea, but all that was built was a section from Chesterfield to Lincoln, together with a branch to Beighton on the GCR route to Sheffield. The Treeton–Brightside line had been originally promoted by the Midland, but in order to gain access into Sheffield, the LD&ECR, backed by the Great Eastern Railway (GER), agreed to build and operate it, with running powers for both the Midland and the GER.

The line opened in 1900 (see map 6), with stations at Catcliffe and Tinsley Road (West Tinsley from 1907), and a service of six LD&ECR trains daily between Sheffield Midland and Langwith Junction on the LD&ECR 'main line'. The Midland added a Sheffield–Mansfield service of four trains a day in 1903. Despite its Midland connections, the line became part of the LNER in 1923, and lost its passenger services in 1939 when the two branch stations closed. The line was virtually unused by 1960, when it was chosen as the site of an £11 million scheme to rationalise freight in the Sheffield area, with a single gigantic

The spectacular Oaks Viaduct was a feature of the Cudworth–Barnsley branch until demolition in 1969. (M.A. King)

marshalling yard and depot at Tinsley. New connections were put in to give northbound access at Treeton and to the former GCR Sheffield–Rotherham line, and the completed yard with a grand total of 89 sidings opened in 1965. Despite cutbacks since the 1980s, this has given the former LD&ECR branch an importance far beyond its sponsors' hopes.

By contrast the Cudworth–Barnsley branch was a purely Midland affair. Dissatisfied with the LYR station facilities at Barnsley, the Midland built its own temporary station there in 1869 (replaced by Court House station three years later), and linked it to its main line at Cudworth with a 4½-mile branch (see map 8). An intermediate station was provided at Monk Bretton in 1876, although the line's main feature was the 1,087-ft Oaks Viaduct which crossed two railways, a main road, a river and two canals! The line was worked by a shuttle service from Barnsley connecting with the main-line trains at Cudworth. This was later nicknamed the 'pusha' and reached a peak in 1912, with twenty trains each way Mondays–Fridays, with an

138

The West Riding Lines extension required several major viaducts, including this fine example, which still survives at Horbury Bridge. (Author)

The Midland's intended Dewsbury station site was still in use as a goods terminus in 1964. (Stations UK)

extra two on Saturdays and seven on Sundays. However, Monk Bretton station closed in 1937, and the shuttle service ended in 1958. The Oaks Viaduct was demolished in 1969, and now the only remnant of the branch is the half-mile single-track spur to Monk Bretton glassworks.

The Midland's Royston–Thornhill line was intended to be far more than an underused link. In 1898 the West Riding Lines Act was passed for new lines to Huddersfield, Halifax and Bradford. Work started at Royston in 1902 and the line to Thornhill was finished within three years. A goods link was built from Mirfield to Huddersfield Newtown in 1910, but the grandiose plans for passenger operations there and especially for the line to Bradford, which would have provided that city with a route across its centre, were finally abandoned in 1919. The Royston–Thornhill line was built to the highest standards, but its two stations at Crigglestone and Middletown only handled freight, with no passenger traffic. Only a Halifax–Sheffield service and a few through trains ever used the line, notably St Pancras–Bradford expresses and the Marylebone–Bradford 'Yorkshireman' between 1927 and 1939. Most passenger services on the line ended in 1948, though summer trains ran until final closure in 1968. Now only the magnificent viaducts at Calder Grove and Horbury Bridge remain as monuments to the Midland's grand ambitions.

9

The Last Contender – the Hull & Barnsley Railway

Kirk Smeaton–Cudworth/
Branches to Denaby and Wath

The last surviving H&B locomotive, the LNER's class N13 0–6–2T no 69114, seen here at Neville Hill shed, Leeds, shortly before withdrawal in 1956. (Author's collection)

Kirk Smeaton–Cudworth

The Hull & Barnsley Railway (H&B) was set up in 1879 to challenge the NER's monopoly of railways to and from the port of Hull. Its 53-mile main line was ruinously expensive to build, the final cost of nearly £6 million being almost three times the

141

Kirk Smeaton was the furthest west of the grand design of H&B stations and still survives as a residence. (Author)

By contrast all the H&B managed at Cudworth was a low single-storey station building shown here on the right in 1950 when it was still used to sign-on guards. (Author's collection)

original estimate. Much of this was due to the difficult route across the hills in East Yorkshire, the Yorkshire Wolds, which required three tunnels and numerous cuttings. However, it is the western section, twelve miles from Kirk Smeaton to Cudworth, that will be dealt with here, and which also contributed to the excessive construction costs of the line, with the 1,226-yard Barnsdale Tunnel and 685-yard Brierley Tunnel among the engineering difficulties.

A lack of outlets in this western section proved crucial. The primary aim was always the movement of coal from South Yorkshire to Hull, where the company built the Alexandra Dock, which, like the railway, opened in 1885. However, at this time the H&B only served two collieries that did not already have access using other railway companies. In addition, its attempt to establish a significant passenger service was ended by the failure to reach Barnsley. A proposed agreement with the Midland for running powers over the lines into that town was rejected in the House of Lords, and the H&B had to make do with a rather ignominious western terminus at Cudworth, four miles to the east. Even this was by courtesy of the Midland, which built an H&B station on an additional platform at its Cudworth station. The H&B paid £20,000 for this and a footbridge to connect it to the rest of the station, but refused a refreshment room for an extra £600. Its station remained a rather mean-looking single-storey building, unlike the quite grand stations built in East Yorkshire. Other stations on this section were at Kirk Smeaton, Upton & North Elmsall and Hemsworth & South Kirkby (1891).

Passenger services began on 27th July 1885, with six weekday trains each way between Cudworth and Hull Cannon Street and one return journey on Sundays. Two years later this was down to five on weekdays, as compared with 28 goods trains, and the disparity for receipts was even greater, with £14,058 from passengers January–June 1900, as against £174,043 from freight. By then exchange sidings at Carlton, more connections to local collieries, and a three-mile freight-only link to the GCR at Stairfoot had all boosted goods traffic.

143

LNER Sentinel railcar no 225 Ebor *was used on services between Cudworth and Kirk Smeaton in the 1920s. (Author's collection)*

It was 1905 before improvements for passengers were implemented. In that year the H&B closed its own Cudworth station and began using the Midland platforms. Running powers had been agreed, so that H&B could put on an express service of four trains a day to and from Sheffield (one on Sundays from 1907). Five new 4-4-0 engines and 'comfortable' bogie coaches were acquired, but the service only lasted twelve years, ending in 1917. By the following year the Cudworth–Hull weekday trains were reduced to two, but the service survived the takeover of the H&B by the NER in 1922. However, final withdrawal of passenger trains over the former H&B line into Cudworth came on 1st January 1932.

Passenger services on the East Yorkshire section of the line continued until 1955, and three years later the last through coal train ran hauled by ex-WD 2–8–0 no 90352, although the line east from Cudworth did not finally close until 1967. Today little is left of the route, especially its westernmost eight miles, most of which have completely disappeared; even much of the Brierley Tunnel is now used for a road, although the station house at Hemsworth & South Kirkby survives. Further east there are cuttings and embankments, plus the fine example of an H&B station at Kirk Smeaton.

Branches to Denaby and Wath

In the 1880s the H&B had grandiose plans to reach Halifax and Huddersfield, but nothing came of them, and these two branches were the only extensions that were ever built. First was an eleven-mile branch from Wrangbrook Junction, three miles south-west of Kirk Smeaton, to the mines at Cadeby and Denaby. It was the colliery company that proposed and built the line, using the name South Yorkshire Junction Railway, although it was operated from the outset by the H&B. This was primarily a freight line, but stations were built at Pickburn & Brodsworth, Sprotborough, and Denaby & Conisbrough, and a passenger service operated from the year of opening, 1894. Two trains each weekday ran between Denaby and Carlton, ten miles further east along the H&B main line from Kirk Smeaton. Within a year withdrawal of this service was proposed, but it lasted until 1903. The branch then concentrated on freight for another 64 years, with miners' trains as required and, in later years, enthusiasts' railtours. The last of these was in 1965, and two years later most of the branch closed. The Denaby end continued in use into the 1970s, with the link, put in by the GCR across the River Don, the last to close in 1981. Little is left of the line, but while the other two stations have disappeared, Sprotborough still survives today.

Wrangbrook Junction was also the starting point for the eight-mile H&B branch to Wath. This began as the independent Hull & South Yorkshire Extension Railway in 1897, but was taken over by the H&B the next year. Although this line too was primarily concerned with the movement of coal, its passenger services were more numerous and lasted longer than those on

Sprotborough station in the early years of the 20th century. (Author's collection)

The Sprotborough station building still just about surviving in 2006. (Author)

Wath (H&B) in 1950, when the station building on the left looked unlikely to survive. (Author's collection)

However, a view taken from the opposite direction shows both buildings still in use as residences in 2006. (Author)

the Denaby branch. When the branch opened in 1902, there were five trains on weekdays between the H&B station at Wath and Kirk Smeaton, which was rebuilt with an extra bay platform for this service. In addition there were another six Monday–Friday trains from Wath to one of the line's two intermediate stations at Hickleton & Thurnscoe (the other was at Moorhouse & South Elmsall). Twenty years later the branch was still quite busy with seven weekday trains, helped by the close proximity of the GCR station at Wath, which provided connections for Barnsley and Doncaster. However, regular passenger services ended in 1929, although excursions to the coast continued for another ten years. Final closure came in stages, with all the line gone by 1964. Like the Denaby branch, little remains to be seen except for the surviving station buildings at Wath.

Conclusion

A 19th-century illustration shows a magnificent viaduct, with an inset of details of its graceful piers. It was to have been built at Salterhebble to carry the Hull & Barnsley Railway's extension to Huddersfield and Halifax. Neither extension nor viaduct was ever built, but they show the lengths to which competing railway companies were prepared to go to serve the former West Riding. It is unlikely that either town missed this particular project, as both were already served by two companies, which would have been three in the case of Huddersfield had the Midland's equally ambitious plans for the expansion of its passenger services been realised.

So was such duplication of routes responsible for the closures in the area covered by this book? Undoubtedly, in some cases – the Spen Valley towns hardly required two stations each, nor Wath-on-Dearne three, all built by different companies. Yet these examples have now all disappeared, suggesting that more than just over-provision of routes was behind the closures. The table of these lines' opening and closure dates suggests a distinct pattern. Most early closures were the branches hardest hit by competition from trams, as at Rothwell and Birstall. After the Grouping, the LMS and LNER axed some of their loss-making branches, particularly in the Calder Valley and east of Barnsley. Most remaining semi-rural branches closed early in BR days, along with a couple of through routes (Askern and Pickle Bridge) and the last of the coalfield branches (Dearne Valley). At this time there were definite attempts to reduce duplication with closures including the ex-GCR Barnsley–Sheffield line, the Leeds New Line, and most contentiously the Queensbury lines. All this was pre-Beeching; around three-quarters of the line closures (to passengers) in this area were before 1963. In fact the Beeching Report only resulted in seven closures, with another five since the 1960s. It is these later cases that provoke most controversy, most notably in the case of Woodhead, but also in terms of Bradford being left with main line access only through Leeds, and the towns of the Spen and Dearne valleys with no railways at all.

It is not the purpose of this book to examine the case for and against closure in any of these examples, but the above summary does suggest an interesting line of thought. It could be argued that, apart from a surprisingly small number of instances of duplication, the railway network as it was in, say, 1895, adequately reflected the needs of the area in an age when the only alternatives were horse-drawn. Only with the introduction of the electric tram, and then the ever-growing dependence on the lorry, bus and car, did increasing parts of the network become superfluous. As this happened lines were closed, not in a 1960s purge as in other parts of the country, but in a steady progression over around 80 years. The question remains – did the closures go too far, especially for years to come when transport priorities may well change?

In the meantime, there is much left to enjoy from the 'Age of the Railway'; ranging from the branch-line experience of the K&WVR, to the lengths of former trackbed now used for the Trans Pennine Trail. While other physical remains are perhaps not as plentiful as in other areas, there are still enough one-time stations, viaducts, tunnels and walkable trackbeds left to make a visit to many of these former lines worthwhile. It is hoped that this book will help in commemorating what is left of the area's railway heritage, as well as providing some explanation of how it came to be.

Dates of Opening and Final Closure of Lines to Regular Passenger Traffic

Line	Opened	Final Closure
Swinton–Cudworth–Normanton	1.7.1840	4.10.1982
Dunford Bridge–Penistone	14.7.1845	5.1.1970
Penistone–Sheffield	14.7.1845	16.5.1983
Knottingley–Askern Junction	6.6.1848	27.9.1948
Mirfield–Heckmondwike–Low Moor	18.7.1848	14.6.1965
Holmfirth branch	1.7.1850	2.11.1959
Mexborough–Barnsley	1.7.1851	5.1.1970
Birstall branch	30.9.1852	1.1.1917
Laisterdyke–Morley–Ardsley	10.10.1857*	4.7.1966
Barnsley–Sheffield (GCR)	1.8.1864*	7.12.1953[1]
Wakefield–Batley–Adwalton Junction	15.12.1864*	7.9.1964[2]
Arthington–Otley–Burley	1.8.1865*	22.3.1965
Dewsbury (Market Place) branch	1.4.1867	1.12.1930
Keighley & Worth Valley Railway	15.4.1867	1.1.1962[3]
Kirkburton branch	7.10.1867	28.7.1930
Methley Joint Railway	1.5.1869	2.11.1964
Heckmondwike–Thornhill	1.6.1869	1.1.1962
Meltham branch	5.7.1869	23.5.1949
Cudworth–Monk Bretton–Barnsley	2.5.1870	9.6.1958
Tinsley–Rotherham–Mexborough	3.4.1871*	5.9.1966
Stainland branch	1.1.1875	23.9.1929
Laisterdyke–Shipley (GNR)	15.4.1875	2.2.1931
Cross Gates–Wetherby	1.5.1876	6.1.1964
Stanningley–Pudsey	1.4.1878	15.6.1964

Garforth–Ledston–Castleford	12.8.1878	22.1.1951
Bradford–Queensbury	14.10.1878[4]	23.5.1955
Clayton West branch	1.9.1879	24.1.1983
Queensbury–Halifax	1.12.1879*	23.5.1955
Ossett–Dewsbury–Batley	12.4.1880*	7.9.1964
Rishworth branch	1.3.1881*	8.7.1929
Pickle Bridge branch	1.3.1881	June 1948
Stairfoot–Nostell	1.9.1882	22.9.1930
Queensbury–Keighley	1.11.1884*	23.5.1955
Kirk Smeaton–Cudworth	27.7.1885	1.1.1932
Batley–Tingley–Beeston	1.8.1890	29.10.1951
Halifax High Level Railway	5.9.1890	1.1.1917
Dudley Hill–Low Moor	1.12.1893	31.8.1914
Wrangbrook Junction–Denaby	1.12.1894	2.2.1903
Brightside–Catcliffe–Treeton	30.5.1900	11.9.1939
Leeds New Line	1.10.1900	5.10.1953
Wrangbrook Junction–Wath	23.8.1902	6.4.1929
Stourton–Rothwell–Robin Hood	4.1.1904	30.9.1904
South Yorkshire Joint Railway	1.12.1910	2.12.1929
Dearne Valley Railway	3.6.1912	10.9.1951

Not included: Royston–Thornhill open for through passenger traffic 1909–1968

Note: Closure dates are those posted by the operating company, usually a Monday, with the last train on the previous Saturday or Sunday. Reopenings by preservation societies have not been included.

* Opened in stages to this date.
1. Tinsley–Sheffield section closed 5.9.1966.
2. The Ossett to Batley via Chickenley Heath section closed to passengers 1.07.1909.
3. Reopened 29.6.1968 by Keighley & Worth Valley Preservation Society.
4. Queensbury station not open until 14.4.1879.

Bibliography

Many of the following are out of print but can still be obtained second-hand or consulted in libraries.

Anderson, Robert *Huddersfield, Dewsbury and Batley* (no 13 in the 'Railway Memories' series published by Bellcode Books)

Bairstow, Martin *The Great Northern Railway in West Yorkshire* (Wyvern Publications)

Bairstow, Martin *The Keighley and Worth Valley Railway* (Martin Bairstow)

Barnett, A.L. *The Railways of the South Yorkshire Coalfield from 1880* (Railway Correspondence and Travel Society)

Batty, S. *Leeds & Bradford* (no 12 in the 'Rail Centres' series originally published by Ian Allan and reissued by Booklaw Publications)

Batty, S. *Sheffield* (no 11 in the 'Rail Centres' series originally published by Ian Allan and reissued by Booklaw Publications)

Chapman, Stephen *The Hull & Barnsley Railway* (no 12 in the 'Railway Memories' series published by Bellcode Books)

Dilmot, John *The Cleckheaton Branch* [LYR Spen Valley line] (no 4 in the 'Branchlines of the LYR' series published by the Lancashire & Yorkshire Railway Society)

Earnshaw, Alan *The Holmfirth (Summer Wine) Branch Line* (Nostalgia Road Publications)

Farline, John and Cookson, Peter *Railways Around Wakefield and Pontefract* (Wyvern Publications)

Fisher, Jeffrey N. *The Rishworth Branch* (Oakwood Press)

Franks, D.L. *East & West Yorkshire Union Railways* (Turntable Enterprises)

Goode, C.T. *Huddersfield Branch Lines* (C.T. Goode)

Goode, C.T. *The Dearne Valley Railway* (C.T. Goode)

Goode C.T. *The Railways of Castleford* (C.T. Goode)

Green D. and Rose P. *Barnsley, Cudworth and Royston* (no 8 in the 'Railway Memories' series published by Bellcode Books)

Johnson E.M. *Woodhead Parts Two and Three* (Foxline Publishing)

Joy, David *South and West Yorkshire* (volume 8 in the 'Regional History of the Railways of Great Britain' series published by David & Charles)

Rockett, Ron *The Leeds, Castleford & Pontefract Junction Railway* (Martin Bairstow)

Ross, Tony *The Dewsbury Branch* [to Market Place station] (no 8 in the 'Branchlines of the LYR' series published by the Lancashire & Yorkshire Railway Society)

Smith, F.W. and Bairstow, Martin *The Otley & Ilkley Joint Railway* (Martin Bairstow)

Waring, Roy *The Leeds New Line* (Oakwood Press)

Whitehouse, Alan *Rails Through Barnsley* (Wharncliffe Publishing)

Whittaker, Alan and Cryer, Bob *The Queensbury Lines* (Dalesman Books)

Wild, Jack *Halifax and the Calder Valley* (no 11 in the 'Railway Memories' series published by Bellcode Books)

A particularly useful website for part of this area is at: www.lostrailwayswestyorkshire.co.uk

Index

155